SELF MASTERY
THROUGH
CONSCIOUS
AUTOSUGGESTION

SELF MASTERY THROUGH CONSCIOUS AUTOSUGGESTION

EMILE COUÉ

WITH INTRODUCTION BY MITCH HOROWITZ

MEDIA

Published 2019 by Gildan Media LLC
aka G&D Media
www.GandDmedia.com

Front cover design by David Rheinhardt of Pyrographx

Interior design by Meghan Day Healey of Story Horse, LLC

Library of Congress Cataloging-in-Publication Data is available upon request

ISBN: 978-1-7225-0263-8

10   9   8   7   6   5   4   3   2   1

Contents

Introduction to this Edition

The Promise of a Forgotten Mind Pioneer

Emile Coué's Unrecognized Genius May Leave You Feeling Better and Better Every Day

By Mitch Horowitz

One of the most significant names in modern psychological and motivational philosophy will evince blank looks from most people today: French mind theorist Emile Coué (1857–1926). Yet Coué, who earned both adulation and jeers during his lifetime, devised a simple, mantra-based method of self-reprograming that has recently been validated across a wide range of disciplines, often by researchers who are unaware of the inceptive insights upon which their studies rest. I believe that Coué's methods not only deserve new credit and respect, but also hold promise for contemporary seekers and anyone in pursuit of practical therapeutic methods.

Coué proposed a simple formula of using mantras or affirmations to reprogram your psyche along the lines of confidence, enthusiasm, and wellness. His methods prefigured the work of self-help giants like Napoleon Hill,

Maxwell Maltz, and Anthony Robbins, as well as recent clinical developments in sleep, neuro, placebo, and psychical research. Indeed, at one time thousands of people in America and Europe swore by Coué's approach. His key mantra—"day by day, in every way, I am getting better and better"—was repeated by The Beatles and a wide range of therapists and spiritual writers. In rediscovering Coué, you will be able to determine for yourself if his simple approach works. It requires only seconds each day.

THE BIRTH OF AN IDEA

Before exploring Coué's method and its application, it is useful to understand his unusual background. Born in Brittany in 1857, Emile Coué developed an early interest in hypnotism, which he pursued through a mail-order course from Rochester, New York. Coué more rigorously studied hypnotic methods in the late 1880s with physician Ambroise-Auguste Liébeault. The French therapist Liébault was one of the founders of the so-called Nancy School of hypnotism, which promoted hypnotism's therapeutic uses. Leaving behind concepts of occultism and cosmic laws, many of the Nancy hypnotists saw their treatment as a practical form of suggestion, mental reprograming, relaxation, and psychotherapy.

This was Coué's view, bolstered by personal experience. While working as a pharmacist at Troyes in northwestern France in the early 1900s, Coué made a startling discovery. Patients responded better to medications when he spoke in praise of the formula. Coué came to believe that the imagination aided not only in recovery but also in a person's general sense of well-being. From this insight, Coué developed his method of "conscious autosuggestion." It was a form of waking hypnosis that involved repeating confidence-building mantras in a relaxed or semiconscious state.

Coué argued that many of us suffer from poor self-image. This gets unconsciously reinforced because your *willpower*, or drive to achieve, is overcome by your *imagination*, by which he meant one's habitual self-perceptions. "When the will and the imagination are opposed to each other," Coué wrote in 1922, "it is always the *imagination* which *wins* . . ." By way of example, he asked people to think of walking across a wooden plank laid on the floor—obviously an easy task. But if the same plank is elevated high off the ground, the task becomes fraught with fear even though the physical demand remains the same. This, Coué asserted, is what we are constantly doing on a mental level when we *imagine* ourselves as worthless or weak.

These insights drove the autosuggestive pioneer toward his signature achievement. Coué believed that through the power of self-suggestion or autosuggestion any individual, with nearly any problem, could self-induce the same kinds of positive results he observed in Troyes. In pursuit of an overarching method, Coué devised his self-affirming mantra: "Day by day, in every way, I am getting better and better." Although few people today have heard of Coué many still recognize his formula. The mind theorist made the phrase famous through lecture tours of Europe and the U.S. in the early 1920s.

To critics, however, Coué reflected everything that was fickle and unsound about modern mind metaphysics and motivational philosophies. How, they wondered, could anyone believe that this singsong little mantra—"day by day, in every way, I am getting better and better"—could solve *anything*? But in a facet of Coué's career that is often overlooked, he demonstrated considerable insight, later validated by sleep researchers and others, in how he prescribed *using* the formula.

Coué said that you must recite the "day by day" mantra just as you're drifting off to sleep at night, when you're hovering within that very relaxed state between wakefulness and sleep. Sleep researchers now call these moments hypnagogia. It is an intriguing state of mind during which you possess sensory awareness, but your perceptions of reality bend and morph, like images from a Salvador Dalí painting. During hypnagogia, your mind is extremely supple and suggestible. Coué understood this by observation and deemed it the period to gently whisper to yourself twenty times: "Day by day, in every way, I am getting better and better." He didn't want you to rouse yourself from your near-sleep state by counting, so he recommended knotting a small string twenty times and then using this device like rosary beads to mark off your repetitions. He also said to repeat the same procedure at the very moment when you wake in the morning, which is sometimes called hypnopompia. It is similar to the nighttime state insofar as you occupy a consciousness shadow world yet possess sufficient cognition to direct your mental workings.

Too Easy to Work?

Coué insisted that his mantra-based routine would reprogram your mind and uplift your abilities. Was he correct? There's one way to find out, at least for your own private purposes: try it. We must never place ourselves above "simple" ideas. I have been influenced the spiritual teacher Jiddu Krishnamurti (1895–1986). He emerged from the Vedic tradition but was an unclassifiable voice. Krishnamurti observed that the greatest impediment to self-development and independent thought is the wish for respectability. Nothing does more to stunt personal experiment, the teacher said, than the certainty that you must follow the compass point of accepted inquiry. Once you grow fixated on that compass point, nearly everything that you read, hear, and encounter gets evaluated on whether it moves you closer to or further from its perceived direction. This makes independent experiment extremely difficult. But if you're unafraid of a little hands-on philosophy, Coué presents the perfect opportunity. He intended his mantra to serve all purposes and circumstances. But you can also craft your own simple mantra that reflects a specific desire. However, you might want to start with Coué's original to get comfortable with the practice.

If you need further encouragement to self-experiment, it may help you to realize that Coué's influence travelled in remarkable directions. The Beatles tried Coué's method and apparently liked it. References to Coué appear in some of their songs. In 1967, Paul McCartney used Coué's mantra in the infectious chorus of *Getting Better*: "It's getting better all the time . . . ," and the lyrics paid further tribute to the healer: "You gave me the word, I finally heard/I'm doing the best that I can." John Lennon recited Coué's formula in his 1980 song *Beautiful Boy*: "Before you go to sleep, say a little prayer: Every day, in every way, it's getting better and better."

Beyond the Fab Four, placebo researchers at Harvard Medical School recently validated one of Coué's core insights. In January 2014, clinicians from Harvard's program in placebo studies published a paper reporting that migraine sufferers responded better to medication when given "positive information" about a drug. This was the same observation Coué had made in the early 1900s. Harvard's study was considered a landmark because it suggested that the placebo response is operative all the time. It was the first study to use suggestion, in this case news about a drug's efficacy, in connection with an active drug rather than an inert substance, and, hence, found that personal expectation impacts how, and to what extent, we experience an active drug's benefits. Although the Harvard paper echoed Coué's original insight, it made no mention of him.*

I wondered whether the researchers had Coué in mind when they designed the study. I asked one of the principals, who did not respond. So, I contacted the director of Harvard Medical School's program in placebo

---

* "Altered Placebo and Drug Labeling Changes the Outcome of Episodic Migraine Attacks" by Slavenka Kam-Hansen, et al, *Science Translational Medicine*, Jan 08, 2014: Vol. 6, Issue 218, pp. 218ra5.

studies, Ted Kaptchuk, a remarkable and inquisitive clinician who also worked on the study. "Of course I know about Coué," Kaptchuk told me. "'I'm getting better day by day . . .'" He agreed that the migraine study coalesced with Coué's observations, though the researchers were not thinking of him when they designed it.

THE INFLUENCE OF AN IDEA

Coué's impact appears under the radar in an unusual range of places. An influential twentieth-century British Methodist minister named Leslie D. Weatherhead looked for a way that patients and seekers could effectively convince themselves of the truth and power of their affirmations, especially when such statements chaffed against circumstantial reality, such as in cases of addiction or persistently low self-worth. Weatherhead was active in the Oxford Group in the 1930s, which preceded Alcoholics Anonymous in pursuit of religious-therapeutic methods. In using suggestions or affirmations to improve one's sense of self-worth and puncture limiting beliefs, the minister was attempting to update Coué.

Weatherhead understood that affirmations—such as "I am confident and poised"—could not penetrate the "critical apparatus" of the human mind, which he compared to "a policeman on traffic duty." Other physicians and therapists similarly noted the problem of affirmations lacking emotional persuasiveness. Some therapists insisted that affirmations had to be credible to get through to the subject; no reasonable person would believe exaggerated self-claims, a point that Coué had also made. While Weatherhead agreed with these critiques, he believed that the rational "traffic cop" could be eluded by two practices. The first was the act of repetition: "A policeman on duty who refuses, say, a cyclist, the first time, might ultimately let him into the town if he presented himself again and again," he wrote in 1951. Continuing the metaphor, Weatherhead took matters further:

> *I can imagine that a cyclist approaching a town might more easily elude the vigilance of a policeman if the attempt to do so were made in the half-light of early dawn or the dusk of evening. Here also the parable illumines a truth. The early morning, when we waken, and the evening, just as we drop off to sleep, are the best times for suggestions to be made to the mind.*

As Weatherhead saw it, the hypnagogic state—again, the drowsy state between wakefulness and sleep, generally experienced when a person is drifting off in the evening or coming to in the morning—is a period of unique psychological flexibility, when ordinary barriers are down. This is pure Couéism. Moreover, this fact probably reflects why people suffering from depression or anxiety report the early waking hours as the most difficult time of day—the rational defenses are slackened. If the individual could use the gentlest efforts to repeat affirmations, without rousing himself fully to a waking state, the new ideas could penetrate, Coué and Weatherhead believed.

The mystical writer Neville Goddard (1905–1972) made a similar point about the malleability of the hypnagogic mind. So did the twentieth-century psychical researcher and scientist Charles Honorton (1946–1992), who used this observation as a basis for testing the potential for telepathy between individuals. Honorton believed that a hypnagogic state was, in effect, "prime time" for the reception of extrasensory communication.

In the early 1970s, Honorton and his collaborators embarked on a long-running series of highly regard psi experiments, known as the *ganzfeld* experiments (German for "whole field"). These trials were designed to induce a hypnagogic state in a "receiver." The subject was placed, seated or reclining, in a soft-lit or darkened room and was fitted with eye covers and earphones, to create a state of comfortable sensory deprivation or low-level stimulation (such as with a "white noise" machine). Seated in another room, a "sender" would attempt to telepathically convey an image to the receiver. After the sending period ended, the receiver was asked to select the correct image among four—three images were decoys, establishing a chance hit-rate of 25 percent. Experimenters found that receivers consistently made higher-than-chance selections of the correct "sent" image. Honorton collaborated with avowed skeptic and research psychologist Ray Hyman in reviewing the data from a wide range of ganzfeld experiments. The psychical researcher and the skeptic jointly wrote: "We agree that there is an overall significant effect in this data base that cannot be reasonably explained by selective reporting or multiple analysis."* Honorton added, "Moreover, we agree that the significant outcomes have been produced by a number of different investigators."

Hyman insisted that none of this was proof of psi, though he later acknowledged that "contemporary ganzfeld experiments display methodological and statistical sophistication well above previous parapsychological research. Despite better controls and careful use of statistical inference, the investigators seem to be getting significant results that do not appear to derive from the more obvious flaws of previous research." Although serious psychical research has come under withering, and often unfair, criticism in recent years, the ganzfeld experiments have remained relatively untouched—and their methodological basis comes from the insights of Coué.

THREE SIMPLE STEPS

Coué's presence emerges, too, in popular literature. One of the most enduring and beguiling pieces of popular metaphysics on the American scene is a 28-page pamphlet called *It Works* written in 1926 by a Chicago ad executive named Roy Herbert Jarrett, who went under the alias R.H.J. Jarrett's widely used method is to write down and focus on your desires—first, you must clarify your need; second, write it down and think of it always; and third, tell no one what you are doing to maintain

---

* "A Joint Communiqué: The Psi Ganzfeld Controversy" by Ray Hyman and Charles Honorton, *Journal of Parapsychology*, vol. 50, December 1986.

mental steadiness. Plain enough, perhaps, but the seeker's insights rested on the deeper aspects of Couéism.

In the early 1920s, Jarrett and many other Americans thrilled to news of Coué's mantra. The "Miracle Man of France" briefly grew into an international sensation as American newspapers featured *Ripley's-Believe-It-Or-Not*-styled drawings of Coué, looking like a goateed magician and gently displaying his knotted string at eye level like a hypnotic device. In early 1923, Coué made a three-week lecture tour of America, making one of his final stops in Jarrett's hometown of Chicago, where the Frenchman spoke at Orchestra Hall.

In a raucous scene, a crowd of more than two thousand demanded that the therapist help a paralytic man who had been seated onstage. Coué defiantly told the audience that his autosuggestive treatments could work only on illnesses that originated in the mind. "I have not the magic hand," he insisted. Nonetheless, Coué approached the man and told him to concentrate on his legs and to repeat, "It is passing, it is passing." The seated man struggled up and haltingly walked. The crowd exploded. Coué rejected any notion that his "cure" was miraculous and insisted that the man's disease must have been psychosomatic.

To some Americans, Coué's message of self-affirmation held special relevance for oppressed people. The pages of Marcus Garvey's newspaper, *Negro World*, echoed Coué's day-by-day mantra in an editorial headline: "Every Day in Every Way We See Drawing Nearer and Nearer the Coming of the Dawn for Black Men."

The paper editorialized that Marcus Garvey's teachings provided the same "uplifting psychic influence" as Coué's.

Coué took a special liking to Americans. He found American attitudes a refreshing departure from what he knew back home. "The French mind," he wrote in 1923, "prefers first to discuss and argue on the fundamentals of a principle before inquiring into its practical adaptability to every-day life. The American mind, on the contrary, immediately sees the possibilities of it, and seeks . . . to carry the idea further even than the author of it may have conceived."

The therapist could have been describing salesman-seeker Roy Herbert Jarrett and many others in the American positive-mind tradition. "A short while ago," Jarrett wrote in 1926, the year of Coué's death, "Dr. Emile Coué came to this country and showed thousands of people how to help themselves. Thousands of others spoofed at the idea, refused his assistance and are today where they were before his visit."

Just as Coué had observed about American audiences, Jarrett boldly expanded on the uses of autosuggestion. Sounding the keynote of the American metaphysical tradition, Jarrett believed that subconscious-mind training did more than just recondition the mind: it activated a divine inner power that served to out-picture a person's mental images into the surrounding world. "I call this power 'Emmanuel' (God in us)," Jarrett wrote. In essence, the entirety of American positive-mind metaphysics rests on Coué-style methods.

*   *   *

Coué's instincts spoke to the individual's profoundest wish for self-help and personal empowerment. It is my observation, as both a historian and seeker, that some people across generations have experienced genuine help through his ideas. So, once more, I invite you to disregard expectation and to self-experiment with Coué's method. We all possess the private agency of personal experiment; indeed, it may be the area in life in which we are most free. Yet we often get so wrapped up in the possibilities of digital culture and the excitement of social media that we neglect the technology of thought, through which we may be able to significantly reform some aspect of ourselves and our surrounding world.

It may be that the ideas of this mind pioneer, a figure so under-recognized in today's culture, offer the very simplicity and effectiveness that you are seeking.

For a brief but complete explanation of how to use the mantra I am providing the words of Emile Coué himself from this 1922 book, *Self Mastery Through Conscious Autosuggestion:*

How to Practice
Conscious Autosuggestion

Every morning on awakening and every evening as soon as you are in bed, close your eyes, and without fixing your attention in what you say, pronounce twenty times, just loud enough so that you may hear your own words, the following phrase, using a string with twenty knots in it for counting:

**"Day by Day, in Every Way,
I am Getting Better and Better."**

The words: "IN EVERY WAY" being good for anything and everything, it is not necessary to formulate particular autosuggestions.

Make this autosuggestion with faith and confidence, and with the certainty that you are going to obtain what you desire.

Moreover, if during the day or night, you have a physical or mental pain or depression, immediately affirm to yourself that you are not going to CONSCIOUSLY contribute anything to maintain the pain or depression, but that it will disappear quickly. Then isolate yourself as much as possible, close your eyes, and pass your hand across your forehead, if your trouble is mental, or over the aching part of your body if physical, and repeat quickly, moving your lips, the words: "IT PASSES, IT PASSES," etc. Continue this as long as may be necessary, until the mental or physical pain has disappeared, which it usually does within twenty or twenty-five seconds. Begin again every time you find it necessary to do so.

Like the first autosuggestion given above, you must repeat this one also with absolute faith and confidence, but calmly, without effort. Repeat the formula as litanies are repeated in church.

*   *   *

MITCH HOROWITZ is a PEN Award-winning historian and the author of books including *Occult America; One Simple Idea: How Positive Thinking Reshaped Modern Life;* and *The Miracle Club: How Thoughts Become Reality.* A lecturer-in-residence at Philosophical Research Society in Los Angeles, Mitch introduces and edits G&D Media's line of Condensed Classics and is the author of the Napoleon Hill Success Course series, including *The Miracle of a Definite Chief Aim, The Power of the Master Mind,* and *Secrets of Self-Mastery.* Follow him @MitchHorowitz

Introduction

The pendulum of medical thought is swinging away from materialism. The day of the predominance of the pill is past. Practitioners of all schools now realize that a very large part of our weal and woe is the result of our thinking. Probably ninety per cent, of all cures have a mental basis independent of the apparent material means employed. This is no argument against the physician or healer of any school, but it is an argument in favor of scientific understanding and employment of mental means for human betterment.

Emile Coué stands out as *leader* of the great and ever increasing host of those who believe that *mind* is the principal factor in health and sickness. He tells us that in every case the material element has its place, but that this place is one of subservience; that matter is servant, *mind is master*; and that matter will obey the direction of mind, if the thing aimed at "is in any way possible." This implies that there may be instances in which the desired thing "is not in any way possible," but Coué does not undertake to define the latter class. After reading of the many cures induced by his "method," one cannot avoid the conclusion that further development and application of the "method" will greatly reduce the field now regarded as "the impossible."

Coué is scientific. He does not start with a theory and then try to prove it by logic; but he begins with "experiments" and builds up his theory inductively. He takes you to a clinic where things are being done, not to a lecture room where things are being discussed. He recognizes the fact that people, not thoroughly acquainted with his "method," may find in it much that "seems childish"; but his answer is, "*it produces results.*" One feels like paraphrasing the words of another: "The lame walk, the ill are made whole, and happy are they who do not stumble at that which is seemingly too simple in my method."

Coué is in line with a considerable number of scholars who have studied and utilized hypnotism in its various phases, particularly related to disease. For many years is was supposed that hypnotism and kindred phenomena were abnormal, but we know now that these phenomena are perfectly natural, that they have been the greatest factors in all the ages for moral and physical health or disease, and that the modern psychologist is merely attempting to use *consciously*, for human good, that which had previously been a great uncontrolled power for both good and ill.

The unique contributions which Coué has made to human betterment are, his recognition of the primary place of the imagination in the cure of disease, and his development of a "method" whereby the imagination may be energized and directed for its beneficent work.

Our mentality is of two sorts, that which we use consciously and that which we use *unconsciously* or subconsciously. Coué agrees with many others in recognizing this dual mentality. But no predecessor, I believe, has recognized the closeness of the relationship between subconscious mentality and the imagination. It would seem, at times, that the two are almost identical in his thought. Is it fair to interpret him as meaning that the imagination is at once the entrance and exit by which we open up our unconscious powers and draw them out for our good or ill? Perhaps so, but he does not theorize much in this little book; his interest is rather in practical cures, and these are so wonderful that the reader will find his credulity put to the test. To this, your natural questioning, Coué and his disciples would say "come and see," which is after all the only scientific test of anything.

The formula, "Every day, in every way, I am getting better and better," Coué says, "covers all cases," and, regardless of the disease or difficulty, this formula repeated as directed produces results if they are "in any way possible." Doubtless the thing which happens is that the imagination takes hold of the general idea of progressive betterment, as suggested in the formula, and fills in the details of that idea with data of its own experience and hope. (The rheumatic patient, repeating the formula, sees himself in imagination reaching the point where he can walk or run, etc.) Now, the wonder of the "method" is this, that this imagined cure has marvelous power to call into action the subjective mind, which produces in reality the thing imagined.

If the Coué "method" has such wonderful effect on the unconscious personality for the cure of disease, why shouldn't it have an effect along moral and social lines that is equally wonderful? The fact seems to be that this process which Coué has learned to utilize for cures, is the process which has been back of every great historic movement. A person gets hold of an idea. He holds it before his imagination until it possesses his subjective mind and transforms him. He constantly gives the thought to others until they are transformed, and eventually the idea of the one man becomes the dominating force of whole nations.

Mr. Coué's brief statement of the relation of his "method" to education is destined to become a classic on this vital subject. That education should begin at birth and even before, that it is the duty of parents and relatives to see to it that the minds of children are placed in the correct attitude toward their own development, that education consists in "self-mastery" and not in teaching subjects; in these matters and some others the "master" stands on common ground with many thoughtful people; but he advances beyond others in showing a clear, scientific, and simple "method" of accomplishing these highly desirable results. The little section in this book which deals with this subject should receive the thoughtful attention of all who are interested in the future of the children of this land.

The name of the originator sometimes leaves its mark in history. Such is Confucius. The history of China for the past twenty-five hundred years is the outworking of the imagination of the Sage in the lives of the untold millions of Chinese through those ages.

Coué has taught us how the psychology of the mob is produced. We are all changed into the image of that which is held before the eyes of our imagination. We can change ourselves as we wish. We can be sick, or well; good, or bad accordingly as we direct our imaginations this way or that. Perhaps we think there are limitations; but let us not talk about those until we have begun to approach them.

We can have the kind of world we want to live in, as soon as we are willing to hold proper ideals before our imaginations until our unconscious minds change us into that which we imagine. And don't forget the night and morning repetition of the *formula*, and even the string with its twenty knots; Coué has proven them to be effective.

ARCHIBALD S. VAN OEDEN

The Miracle Within:
A Tribute to Emile Coué

(Reprint from the "Renaissance Politique, literaire et artistique" of the 18th of December, 1920.)

I n September, 1920, I opened for the first time the book of Prof. Charles Baudouin, of the Institute J. J. Rousseau of Geneva, entitled, *Suggestion and AutoSuggestion*, and dedicated by the author:

"WITH GRATEFUL ACKNOWLEDGMENTS TO EMILE COUÉ, THE STEADFAST WORKER AND PIONEER."

I did not put it down until I had read it through. It contains a very simple exposition of a magnificent humanitarian work, based upon a theory which may appear childish to some, because of its utter simplicity. But if anyone *practices* it he is bound to receive great good from it.

During more than twenty years of indefatigable work, *Emile Coué*, who resides at *Nancy* (where he continued the work and experiments of Liebault, father of the doctrine of suggestion), for twenty years, I repeat, *Coué* studied this one subject, to the exclusion of everything else, for the purpose of helping his fellow creatures by inducing them to cultivate the practice of *autosuggestion*.

At the beginning of this century, *Coué* had attained the object of his researches. He had discovered the immense power of *autosuggestion* and the secret of its application for general use; having made innumerable experiments, with thousands of patients, he *proved* the action of the subconscious on *organic* ailments.

This was something entirely new; and the great merit of this profoundly modest scholar is to have found a remedy for terrible ills, heretofore considered incurable, and without hope of relief, although, in some instances, extremely painful.

As I cannot go into lengthy scientific details, I will just tell how this learned man of *Nancy* practices his method.

The substance of his teaching—clear cut as though in sculpture—found after a lifetime of patient researches, is summed up in a brief formula to be repeated morning and night.

This formula must be repeated in a low voice (with eyes closed, body in a position that permits of relaxing the muscular system—say in bed or in an easy chair) and in a monotonous tone, as if one were reciting a litany. The magic words are:

> **"Every Day, in Every Way,
> I am Getting Better and Better."**

They must be repeated twenty times, morning and night. You may use a string with twenty knots on it which serves as an aid in counting just as a rosary does.

This material aid is important; it insures *mechanical recitation*, which is essential.

While articulating these words which are registered by the *unconscious*, you must not think of anything in particular, neither of your illness nor of your troubles. You must be *passive*, with only the desire that all may be for the best; the formula *in every way* has a general effect.

Your desire must express itself without passion, gently and without exertion of your *will*, but with absolute faith and confidence.

For Emile Coué, at the moment of inducing autosuggestion, *does not appeal to the will in any way. The will must not be exercised at all at that moment! Imagination only* must come into play; that is the great motive power, infinitely more active than the *will power* which is usually invoked.

Have confidence in yourself . . . Believe firmly that all will be well with you, says this great counsellor, and, indeed, *all is well* with those who have the unquestioning faith of a child, supplemented by perseverance.

As facts and deeds speak louder than words, I will tell you of my own experience before I met *M. Coué*.

I must go back to the month of September when I first opened the book of M. Charles Baudouin; after detailed exposition of his subject the author notes complete cures of such maladies as: enteritis; eczema; stammering; dumbness; sinus—dating twenty-five years back, with eleven operations;—metritis; salpingitis; fiberous tumor; varicose veins; etc. etc., and last but not least, deep *tubercular sores* and the last stages of phthisis (as in the case of

Mme. D., of Troyes, age 30, who became a mother after her cure; this case was followed up and there was no relapse). All this is testified to by attending physicians, who had treated the patients.

These examples impressed me profoundly; some were *real miracles!* It was not a question of nerves, but of ills for which there is no medicine as yet. Especially that case of *tuberculosis* was a revelation to me.

Having suffered, myself, horribly from acute neuritis of the face, I know what real pain is. Four physicians, two of them specialists, had pronounced the sentence, "Nothing can be done for you," which, of itself alone, sufficed to increase the trouble by its fatal influence on my mind: That "Nothing can be done" had induced the worst of *autosuggestions*.

Once in possession of the formula: *"Every day, in every way*, etc.," I recited it with a faith, which, although it had come suddenly, was none the less capable of removing mountains. I discarded shawls and comforters and, in wind and rain, went out into the garden bareheaded, murmuring gently: *"I am going to be cured; there will be no more neuritis; it is going away, it will not come back, etc."* I was cured the very next day; there was no more suffering from the abominable complaint, which had not allowed me to take a step out of doors in windy or damp weather, and had made life unbearable. Just imagine my intense joy! Skeptics will say, "It was all nervousness." Obviously, and I will concede to them this first point. But, delighted with the *Coué method*, I tried it for an oedema of the left ankle, resulting from an affection of the kidneys which was said to be incurable. In two days the *oedema* had disappeared. I then treated *fatigue* and mental *depression*, etc. An extraordinary improvement resulted and I had but one idea: to go to *Nancy* and thank my benefactor.

I went and found the excellent man who attracts all by his goodness and simplicity, and he became my friend.

It was indispensable to see him on his own field of action. He invited me to a popular clinic. There I witnessed a *concert of gratitude*—lesions of the lungs, displaced organs, asthma, Pott's disease (!), paralysis—all this host of deadly diseases was put to flight. I saw a paralytic who sat contorted and twisted in a chair, get up and walk. *Coué* had talked to them urging each to have great confidence, an *immense confidence in themselves*. He said, "Learn to cure yourselves; *you can*. I have never cured anybody; *the remedy is within yourselves*. Call upon your spirit; let it act for your mental and spiritual benefit and it will come, it will cure you; you will be strong and happy." Having spoken, *Coué* approached the paralytic and said to her: "You have heard. *Do you believe that you will walk? . . .*" "Yes." . . . "Very well then, *get up!*" The woman arose, she walked, and went around the garden. The miracle was accomplished.

A young girl afflicted with Pott's disease, whose vertebral column had become straight again after three treatments, told me of the intense happiness she felt in being, so to speak, *reborn* after having been a hopeless cripple. Three women, cured of *lesions* of the lungs, expressed delight at being able to go back to work and to enjoy normal life.

Coué, in the midst of these people whom he loves, appeared to me as a person apart; he ignores money; all his work is gratuitous and his extraordinary disinterestedness does not permit him to take a cent for it. I told him: "I owe you something—I owe you all!" His reply was: "No, the pleasure that I have in your continued well-being pays me abundantly."

An irresistible sympathy draws you toward this plain philanthropist who has the soul of a child. Arm in arm we walk around the kitchen-garden, which he cultivates himself getting up early to do so. He is practically a vegetarian and looks upon the results of his garden work with great satisfaction. He then resumes serious conversation. "You possess within you an unlimited power, your *Unconscious being*, commonly called *imagination*. It acts on matter if we but know how to domesticate it. The imagination may be compared to a horse, improperly harnessed to your carriage, and without bridle or reins; that horse may perform all sorts of foolish tricks and cause your death. But, harness him properly, drive him with a firm hand, and he will go where you want him to. It is the same with your *Unconscious self*, your *imagination*. You must direct it for your own good. *Autosuggestion* formulated with the lips, is an order which the Unconscious receives. It carries it out, unknown to ourselves, especially at night; so that the evening suggestion is the most important. It gives wonderful results.

"When you feel physical pain add the formula: *'It passes, it passes.'* Repeat it *very quickly*, in a sort of murmuring voice, placing your hand on the aching part, or upon your forehead if it is mental discomfort or distress. The method also acts very effectively on the mind. After having called in the help of the soul for the body, you can call on it again and again in all circumstances and difficulties of life."

I know from experience that unsatisfactory results, obtained by usual treatment, can be singularly modified by this process.

You now know about it, and can know it still better if you will read Mr. Baudouin's book, "Suggestion and Autosuggestion" and then his pamphlet: "Culture of the Moral Power," after reading this brief little treatise, *"Self-Mastery,"* written by *Mr. Coué* himself.

Now, if I have been able to inspire you sufficiently to make the pilgrimage to *Nancy* for yourself, you will have the same experience that I had; you will love this unique man—unique by reason of his noble charity and his unselfish love of his brethren as Christ has taught it.

And, like myself, you will be *healed* physically, morally and mentally. Life will seem more worth living and altogether more beautiful. And that is surely worth trying for.

Self Mastery: Through Conscious Autosuggestion

By Emile Coué.

Suggestion, or rather, *Autosuggestion* is in one sense an entirely new subject, although, at the same time, it is as old as the world itself.

It is new in that, up to the present, it has not been studied from the correct viewpoint, and consequently wrong conclusions have been formed. It is old because it dates back to the advent of man on Earth. Indeed, *autosuggestion* is an instrument which we possess when we are born. It is a force of wonderful and incalculable power which produces, according to circumstances, the very best or the very worst effects. A proper knowledge of this force is useful to everyone, but, more particularly, it is indispensable to physicians, magistrates, lawyers and educators of the young.

When one knows how to employ it consciously he can, first of all, guard himself against provoking harmful *autosuggestions* in others, the consequences of which may be disastrous; furthermore, he can consciously bring about helpful ones which restore physical health to the sick, and mental and moral vigor to the nervously deranged—unconscious victims of previous hurtful auto-suggestions; he can also guide into right ways those who have a tendency toward evil.

The Conscious Being and the Unconscious Being

In order to understand the phenomena of suggestion or, more accurately, of *autosuggestion*, it is necessary to realize that there exist, within us, two beings absolutely distinct from each other. Both are intelligent, but while one is conscious, the other is *unconscious*. That is the reason why the existence of the latter is not generally recognized.

The existence of this *unconscious* being may be easily proved if one will only take the trouble to examine certain phenomena and to think a little, for example:

Everybody is familiar with somnambulism. We all know that the sleep-walker gets up during the night and, *without being awake*, leaves his room, dressed or undressed, goes downstairs, walks along corridors and, after having performed certain acts or accomplished certain work, returns to bed. Next morning he is greatly astonished at finding work finished which he had left unfinished the night before.

Nevertheless he himself did it, although he does not recall anything about it. What power then did his body obey, if not an unconscious force, his *unconscious being?*

Consider now, if you please, the regrettably frequent case of the drunkard in a state of "delirium tremens." In a paroxysm of rage he takes up whatever weapon is handy, a knife, hammer, axe, and strikes furiously at those who have the misfortune to be near him. When the paroxysm of rage has passed and he regains his senses, he looks with horror at the scene of carnage, ignorant of the fact that he himself did it. Here again, isn't it the unconscious that has directed the actions of the poor wretch?*

If we compare the Conscious with the *Unconscious*, we find that while the Conscious is endowed with a very unreliable memory, the *Unconscious* on the contrary, is gifted with a marvelous memory which registers unfailingly, without our knowing it, every event and every least little thing that happens during our existence. Moreover it is credulous and accepts, without reasoning, what it is told. As the *Unconscious* directs and controls the working of all our organs by the intermediary of the brain an apparently paradoxical effect is produced; that is, when it believes that a particular organ is or is not in proper working order, or that we feel such and such an impression, that organ, indeed, works properly or badly; or rather, we have the impression that it does.

The *Unconscious* not only presides over the functions of our organism but also over the performance of *all our actions*, whatever they may be.

The *Unconscious* is what we usually call "imagination" and which, contrary to the common belief, always

---

* And what aversions, what ills of various degrees, often hardly perceptible, we create in ourselves, all of us, by neglecting to counter-balance immediately the bad *unconscious* autosuggestions, by using good, *conscious autosuggestions*, thus bringing about the cessation of much unnecessary suffering.

makes us act, *even against our will*, if there is antagonism between those two forces.

Will and Imagination

When we open a dictionary and look for the sense of the word *"Will"* we find the following definition: "Faculty to freely determine all our actions." We accept this definition as true and indisputable, but there is no greater fallacy. This *will* which we so proudly assert, always gives way to the imagination. This is an *absolute rule without a single exception.*

Blasphemy! Paradox! You say. Not at all. Truth! Absolute truth, I reply.

And in order to convince yourself of this truth open your eyes, look about you and try to comprehend what you see. You will then understand that what I assert is not an empty theory, engendered by a disordered brain, but the plain expression of an actual fact.

Suppose that we place on the floor a plank 30 feet long and 10 inches wide. It is evident that everybody would be able to walk along that plank from one end to the other without stepping off. Now change the conditions of the experiment and suppose that this plank is placed, let us say, as high as the towers of a cathedral; where then is the person capable of walking only a single foot along that narrow path made by the board? Would *you* who read this be the one? Doubtless *no.* You wouldn't take two steps before you began to tremble and IN SPITE

OF ALL THE EFFORTS OF YOUR WILLPOWER you would certainly tumble to the ground.

Why is it that you do not fall when the plank is on the ground? And how is it that you do fall when it is raised to any great height? Simply because in the first case you *imagine that it is easy* to walk to the end of that plank, while in the second case you *imagine that it is impossible*.

Observe that you may *will* to walk along it, as much as you please, but, if you imagine *that you cannot*, it is absolutely impossible for you to do it.

Dizziness is caused by the *image formed in our minds* that we are going to fall. This *image* transforms itself immediately into the *act*, IN SPITE OF ALL EFFORTS OF OUR WILL, and even the more quickly the more violent our will-efforts are to the contrary.

Let us consider the case of a person afflicted with insomnia. If he makes no effort to sleep, he will rest quietly in his bed. If, on the contrary, he "wants" to sleep, the greater his efforts to go to sleep the more restless he becomes.

Have you ever noticed the fact that the more you try to remember the name of a person which, for the moment, you have forgotten, the harder it becomes for you to recall, until you dismiss the thought "I have forgotten" and think instead "it will come back to my mind"; then the name comes to you naturally and without the least effort?

Those who ride bicycles will readily recall their first efforts. While holding on tightly to the handlebars for fear of a fall, suddenly you observe in the road a harmless little pebble or perhaps even a horse. You try to avoid the obstacle but, the more you try to avoid it, the straighter you go right to it.

Who has not, at one time or another had an uncontrollable fit of laughter that became more uncontrollable with each effort to suppress it?

What was the state of mind of each of these persons? "I do not want to fall but *I can't help it*. I WANT TO sleep but *cannot*. I would like to remember the name of Madame A., but I *cannot*. I WANT to avoid that obstacle but *cannot*. I WANT to suppress that laugh, but I *cannot*."

You will readily see that in each case, though under different circumstances, it was *always the imagination that carried away the will*, without a single exception.

Similarly, we note an officer rushing forward at the head of his troops; his courageous example inspires them to follow; but the cry: "Save yourselves" causes a disorderly and fatal retreat. WHY? In the first case, the *men imagine that they must march forward* and, in the second, they *imagine that they are beaten* and must flee to escape death.

Panurge knew the contagion of example, or the force of imagination, when, to take revenge on a merchant with whom he sailed, he seized and threw overboard his biggest sheep, sure in advance, that the whole herd would follow; which of course happened.

We human beings, resemble more or less a flock of sheep. Against our will we follow the example of others, *imagining* that we cannot do otherwise.

I could cite thousands of other examples, only the enumeration would be tiresome. I cannot, however, omit emphasizing this factor of the enormous power of imagination, otherwise called the *Unconscious*, in its fight against the *will*.

Drunkards would gladly stop drinking but they cannot control themselves. Ask them. They will tell you, in all sincerity, that they would like to be abstemious, that drink is disgusting to them, but that they are irresistibly driven to drink, in spite of their Will, and in spite of the evil consequences which they *know* are sure to result.

In the same manner criminals commit crimes *in spite of themselves*. When you ask them why they have acted that way, they reply: "I could not help myself, I was pushed to it, it was beyond my power of resistance."

And the drunkard as well as the criminal speaks the truth: They are forced to act as they do because they *imagine* that they cannot help themselves.

I do not say that your *will* is not a power. On the contrary, it is a great force; but it almost always turns against you. Your state of mind must be: "I desire to do (or to have) such and such a thing and I am about to do (or to have) it." If you make no *will-efforts* you will succeed.

Now then, we who are so proud of our *willpower*; we who think that we act *voluntarily*; we are, *in reality*, only poor puppets directed by our *imagination* which holds the reins. We cease to be puppets only after we have learned to consciously direct our imagination.

Suggestion and Autosuggestion

We may properly compare the *imagination* to a torrent which carries to destruction the unlucky one who gets into its current, even in spite of his *will* and efforts to reach shore. This torrent appears indomitable. But if you know how, you may turn it from its course, divert it, as it were, to the factory, and transform its force into useful driving power, heat and electricity.

Again, we may liken the *imagination* to a wild horse with neither bridle nor reins. What else can the rider do but to let the horse carry him where it will? Then, if the horse stumbles, the rider plunges into the ditch which stopped its mad career. But consider, if the rider puts bridle and reins on the horse and breaks it to harness, the roles are changed. The horse no longer goes wherever it wants to; it is the *rider* who now controls and directs all its movements.

What is *suggestion?* One could define it as "the act of imposing an idea on the brain of another person." Is such an action really possible? Properly speaking, no. Suggestion does not actually exist by itself. It does not exist, and cannot exist except on the distinct condition, *sine qua non*, that it *transforms itself* in the other person's mind *into autosuggestion*: and this word we define as *"implanting an idea in one's self through one's self."*

You may suggest something to someone. If the *Unconscious* of the latter does not accept that suggestion, if he does not digest it, so to speak, and transform it into *autosuggestion*, no effect is produced.

It has happened to me, occasionally, that suggestions, more or less commonplace, when given to ordinarily obedient patients, have failed entirely. The reason was that the *Unconscious* of those patients refused to accept the suggestions and did not transform them into *autosuggestions*.

The Use of Autosuggestion

Return now to the point where I said that we could control and direct our *imagination* as easily as we could divert a torrent or control a wild horse. All that is required is for us *to realize that it is possible*, a fact of which most people are ignorant. Next, we must know what *means* to use. Well, the means are very simple. In fact, without wanting to and without knowing it, we have employed them absolutely *unconsciously* every day since we came into the world; but, unfortunately for us, we have often employed them wrongly and to our disadvantage. The means are, AUTOSUGGESTIONS.

Instead of autosuggesting unconsciously, all that is needed is for us to *autosuggest consciously*, and here is the way to do it: first consider carefully the things which are to be the object of your autosuggestions and decide whether the matters require an affirmation or a negation; then repeat several times, without *thinking of anything else*: "this comes" or "this goes"; this is going to happen or that is not going to happen, etc., etc. If the *Unconscious* accepts the suggestion, if it *autosuggests*, you will find that the idea is realized in every detail.

Please understand that *autosuggestion* is nothing else but hypnotism as I comprehend it, and may be defined in simple words as *influence of the imagination on the moral and physical being of man*. This influence is undeniable and, without repeating examples previously noted I will cite several others.

If you induce in yourself a belief that you can do a certain thing (provided it conforms to the laws of nature) you are going to do it, no matter how difficult it may be. If, on the contrary, you imagine that you cannot do the simplest thing in the world, it becomes impossible for you to accomplish it. A mole-hill may become to you an unsurmountable mountain.

This, particularly, is the case of neurasthenics who, believing themselves incapable of the slightest effort, find it impossible even to take only a few steps, without suffering extreme fatigue. And these same neurasthenics, by their very efforts to rid themselves of their depression, only get deeper and deeper into it, like the unfortunate who gets into quicksand and sinks deeper and deeper, the more energetically he struggles to free himself.

In like manner it suffices just *to think* that a pain is going to cease in order to feel that the pain does actually disappear little by little, and, vice versa, it suffices just *to think* that you are suffering, to immediately feel the pain coming.

I know some persons who can predict in advance that they are going to have a headache on such and such a day, under certain circumstances; and on that day, the circumstances occurring, they have their headaches. They cause themselves pain, while others get rid of theirs by *conscious autosuggestion.*

I am well aware that, speaking generally, one is considered a fool who dares to develop entirely new ideas. Well then! Even at the risk of being called a fool I say that if some folks are mentally or physically sick, it is because they *imagine* themselves to be sick, either mentally or physically. And that, if some folks are paralytics, without a lesion of any kind, they simply *imagine* that they are paralyzed. Among this class of people most extraordinary cures have been effected.

If others are happy or unhappy, it is because they *imagine* themselves to be happy or unhappy. It is possible for two people, in exactly similar circumstances and conditions, to become, the one perfectly happy and the other absolutely miserable.

Neurasthenia, stammering, fear of the water, kleptomania, certain forms of paralysis, etc., are nothing else but the result of the action of the *Unconscious* upon the physical, mental or moral being.

But if the *Unconscious* is the source of many of our ills and ailments it can also bring about the cure of our mental or physical afflictions. It can not only repair the evil it has done, but also cure real maladies, so great is its action on our organism.

Isolate yourself in a room; sit down in an easy-chair; *close your eyes* to avoid all distraction and think exclusively for a few moments: "Such and such a thing is going to disappear," or "such and such a thing is going to happen."

If you have *really autosuggested*, that is, if your *Unconscious* has absorbed the idea which you have suggested, then you will be astonished to see happen the very thing your mind dwelt upon. (It is to be noted that it is the property of ideas *autosuggested* to exist within us unrecognized. We only know of their existence by the effects they produce.) Above all, this is an essential point: THE WILL MUST NOT BE BROUGHT INTO PLAY IN PRACTISING AUTOSUGGESTION because, if it is not in accord with the imagination, if one thinks: "I *will* such and such a thing to happen" and the *imagination* says: "You are *willing* it, but it is not going to be," you will not only NOT obtain what you want, but moreover, exactly the opposite may happen.

This observation is of *utmost importance*, and explains why results are so little satisfactory when, in treating moral ailments, one strives *to re-educate the will*. It is the training of the *imagination* which is necessary and it is due to this difference that my method has often succeeded where other methods have failed.

The numerous experiments which I have made, daily, for twenty years, and which I have observed most carefully, have enabled me to arrive at the following conclusions, which I have summed up as LAWS:

1. When the will and the imagination are opposed to each other, it is always the *imagination* which *wins, without any exception whatever.*

2. In the conflict between the will and the imagination, *the force of the imagination is in direct ratio to the square of the will.*

3. When the will and the imagination are in accord, one does not add to the other, but *one is multiplied by the other.**

4. The imagination can be *directed*.

From what has been said it would seem that nobody should ever be ill. This, is quite true. Every illness, ALMOST WITHOUT EXCEPTION, can be made to yield to *autosuggestion*, however bold and however daring my affirmation may seem. I do not say that it always DOES yield, but that it CAN BE MADE TO yield, which is different.

But in order to get people to practice *autosuggestion* consciously, it is necessary to teach them how, just as they are taught to read or write or to play a musical instrument.

Autosuggestion, as I stated before, is an instrument that is in us at birth, and on which we play unconsciously all our life as a baby plays with a rattle. But it is a dangerous instrument; it can wound or even kill you, if you handle it imprudently and unconsciously. On the other hand it may save your life if you know how to employ it *consciously*. One may say of it what Aesop said of the tongue: "It is the best, and at the same time, the very worst thing in the world."

----

* The expressions "in direct ratio to the square of the will" and "is multiplied" are not rigorously exact. They are used simply as illustrations intended to make my meaning clearer.

How Suggestion Works

I will now explain to you what must be done in order that everybody may enjoy the beneficent action of *auto-suggestion*, applied consciously: In saying "everybody" I exaggerate a little, for there are two classes of people in whom it is difficult to arouse *autosuggestion*.

1. The *mentally deficient* who are unable to understand what you are saying to them.
2. Those who are UNWILLING to understand.

In order to thoroughly understand the part played by suggestion, or rather *autosuggestion*, it is sufficient to know that THE UNCONSCIOUS SELF IS THE GRAND DIRECTOR OF ALL OUR FUNCTIONS. Make the *Unconscious* believe, as I have said above, that a certain organ which does not function as it should, *must perform* its function well, and immediately the order is transmitted. The organ obeys *willingly* and either at once or, little by little, it will function normally again.

This explains simply and clearly how, by means of suggestion, one can stop hemorrhages, cure constipation, cause fibrous tumors to disappear, cure paralysis, tubercular lesions, varicose sores, etc.

For example: take a case of dental hemorrhage, which I had opportunity to observe at the clinic of Dr. Gauthé, dentist at Troyes. A young woman whom I had helped to cure herself of asthma (from which she had suffered for eight years) told me one day that she wanted a tooth pulled. As I knew her to be very sensitive, I offered to make the extraction painless. Naturally, she accepted with pleasure. On the appointed day we called at the dentist's; placing myself opposite the young woman, I looked at her fixedly and said: *You feel nothing, you feel nothing, etc.*; while continuing my suggestion I signalled the dentist; in a moment the tooth was out and Miss D. had noticed nothing; she had not even blinked an eyelash. As happens often, a hemorrhage from the gums followed. Instead of employing a haemostatic I told the dentist that I would try *suggestion*, without knowing beforehand what would happen. I then requested Miss D. to look at me fixedly, and I suggested to her that in two minutes the hemorrhage would stop of its own accord; then we waited; the young woman spat blood again, once or twice, and then it ceased; I asked her to open her mouth; the dentist and I looked, and found that a clot of blood had formed in the cavity.

How is this phenomenon to be explained? In the simplest manner. Under the influence of the idea, *the hemorrhage has got to stop*, the *Unconscious* had sent to the arteries and small veins the order not to allow any more blood to escape and, obediently, they contracted NATURALLY, just as they would have done artificially on contact with a haemostatic, like adrenalin for example.

The same method of reasoning explains how it is possible to cause a fibrous tumor to disappear. The *Unconscious*, having accepted the idea that *the tumor must go*, the brain orders the arteries, which nourish and feed it, to contract. They do contract; they refuse their services to feed the tumor any longer, and deprived of nourishment, it dies, dries up, is reabsorbed, and disappears.

Neurasthenia, so frequent these days, usually yields to suggestion, if constantly practised in the way I have indicated. I have had the satisfaction of contributing to the recovery of many neurasthenics, after every other treatment had failed. One had spent a month in a special sanitarium at Luxemburg, without the least improvement. In six weeks he was completely cured, and he is to-day the happiest man in the world, after having considered himself the most miserable. And he will never have a relapse because I have taught him how to make *conscious autosuggestions*, and he practices them wonderfully well.

The Use of Suggestion for the Cure of Moral Ailments and Congenital or Acquired Faults

But if suggestion is useful in the treatment of mental and physical defects, how much greater service can it render to society in transforming into honest folks the poor, wretched children who now fill our reformatories and who only leave them to join the army of criminals?

Let no one say that this is impossible. It *is possible* and I can prove it! Take the two following cases which are very characteristic. But, parenthetically, to make perfectly clear the manner in which suggestion acts in cases of moral taints, I will use the following comparison. Let us suppose our brain to be a plank with nails driven into it to represent ideas, habits, and instincts which determine our actions. If we observe that there exists in an individual a bad idea, a bad habit, a bad instinct—in a word a bad nail, we take another representing the good idea, the good habit, the good instinct and, placing it on top of the bad nail, give it a tap with a hammer. In other words: we make a *suggestion*. The new nail will be driven in perhaps a fraction of an inch, while the old one will be forced out to the same extent. At each fresh blow with the hammer, that is to say, at each fresh *suggestion*, the new nail will go in another fraction of an inch, and the bad one will be forced out that much further, until, after a sufficient number of blows, the old nail will be driven out entirely and the new one will occupy its place. When this substitution has been made, the individual is governed by the new and correct idea, habit or instinct.

To return to my examples: Little M., a child of 11 years, living at Troyes, was subject to certain little accidents customary in infancy. He was also a kleptomaniac and, of course, untruthful. At his mother's request I treated him by *suggestion*. After the very first treatment those accidents ceased during daytime, but continued at night; little by little they became less frequent and finally, after a few months, the child was completely cured; the impulse to steal was also lessened and, at the end of six months, ceased entirely.

The brother of this child, aged 18, had conceived a violent hatred against another one of his brothers. Every time the elder one had taken a little too much wine, he felt an impulse to draw a knife and stab his brother. He had the feeling that, some day, he would actually commit such a crime, and he knew at the same time that if he did, he would be inconsolable.

I treated him also, by *suggestion*, and the result was marvelous. After the first treatment he was cured. The hatred of his brother vanished completely and they became fast friends. I followed up the case for a long time: the cure was permanent.

Since it is possible to obtain such results by *suggestion*, would it not seem useful, or rather INDISPENSABLE, to introduce this method into houses of correction? I am absolutely certain that, by daily *suggestions* applied to vicious children, more than half could be reformed. Would it not be of great service to society to save and bring back, hale and hearty, members of the human family who were formerly morally, mentally, and physically diseased?

It may be said, perhaps, that suggestion is a dangerous thing and that it might be abused for evil purposes. Such an objection should not be considered as valid. First of all, the *practice of suggestion* would be entrusted to responsible and honorable persons, for instance—to *physicians* attending houses of correction. Secondly, those who would use suggestion for their own evil ends would ask nobody's permission, anyway.

However, admitting for a moment that there might be some danger (which is NOT the case), I would ask the objector to tell me what things we use daily, are not dangerous: how about steam? gunpowder? railroads? ships? electricity? automobiles? aeroplanes? And the poisons which we, doctors and chemists, use every day in infinitesimal doses—might they not kill our patients, if by inattention we make mistakes in weighing them out?

The "Method" Applied to the Education and Correction of Children

By Emile Coué.

Before going further let me say a few words as to the manner of applying my "method," by parents, in the education and correction of children.

Education Should Begin Before Birth

It may appear paradoxical to you but, nevertheless, the education of a child should begin *before birth*.

As a matter of fact, if a prospective mother, a few weeks after conception, will make a mental picture of the child she expects to bring into the world, concerning its sex and the physical and moral qualities with which she desires her offspring to be endowed, and if she will then continue to hold that mental image during the time of gestation, the child will have the sex and qualities desired.

Spartan women brought forth robust children who became redoubtable warriors, because their strongest desire was to give to their country only such sons as were likely to become heroes; while at Athens, the women gave birth to children whose intellectual qualities far surpassed their physical attributes.

A child, thus conceived, will more readily accept good suggestions and transform them into *autosuggestions* which may determine the course of its life. For you must realize that all our words and all our acts are but the results of autosuggestions induced, for the most part, through suggestion by means of example or speech.

What and How to Teach

What then, should parents and teachers do to prevent bad autosuggestions and induce children to make good autosuggestions instead? In dealing with children, always be even-tempered and speak to them in gentle but firm tones. In this way you influence them to be obedient without arousing the slightest desire to resist authority. Above all, be very careful to avoid brutality or harshness, because you risk creating in them autosuggestions of fear accompanied by hate. Furthermore, avoid making damaging or evil remarks about anyone in the presence of children, as often happens in the drawing room, when, without deliberate intention, the nurse or an absent friend is picked to pieces. It follows inevitably that they will imitate your bad example, which may be productive of serious consequences later on.

As soon as children are able to talk, make them repeat morning and evening, twenty times, the words:

Every day, in every way, I am getting better and better. This habit will produce excellent health—physical, mental and moral.

Awaken in them a desire for knowledge and love of nature and endeavor to interest them by giving all possible explanations very clearly, in cheerful, good tempered tones. You must answer their questions pleasantly, instead of checking them roughly with: "What a bother you are . . . do be quiet . . . you will learn that later, etc."

Never, on any account say to children: "You are lazy and good-for-nothing"; because, by so doing, you will create in them the very faults which you reproach them with. If a child is lazy and always does badly what he has to do, you should say to him sometime, even if it is not entirely justified by his actions: "Ah! You have done much better to-day than you usually do; well done, sonnie." The child will feel flattered by such unaccustomed praise and certainly work much better the next time and, little by little, with proper encouragement, will become an earnest worker.

Avoid speaking of sickness before children, as doing so will certainly serve to create in them bad *auto-suggestions*. Teach them, on the contrary, that health is the normal state of man and that sickness is an anomaly, a sort of drawback, which can be avoided by living temperate well regulated lives.

Do not develop weaknesses by teaching them to fear this or that, the cold, the heat, the rain, the wind, etc. Man is created to endure such vicissitudes without injury, without suffering and without complaining.

Do not make children nervous by filling their minds with ideas of hob-goblins, and other fearful things, for there is always the risk that timidity, instilled in child-hood, will persist throughout life.

Those who do not bring up their children them-selves, should be very careful in selecting the people to whom they entrust them. It is not enough that those persons are fond of children; it is necessary that they should also have the very qualities which you desire your children to have.

Awaken in the children a love of work and study. Make it easier for them by explaining, as I said before, clearly and in a pleasant manner, the aim and object of their work and study; introduce, if possible, anecdotes which interest children and make them eager for the les-son that is to follow.

Impress upon them, *above all*, that *work is essential for man* and that he or she who does not do work of one kind or another, is a useless, worthless creature. Impress upon them that all work produces in the man who does it, a wholesome and profound satisfaction; while *idleness*, which appears so desirable to many, produces weariness, neurasthenia, disgust with life; leading those who have not the means of satisfying passions created by idleness, to debauchery and crime.

Teach your children always to be polite and amia-ble towards all, especially to those whom the accident of birth may have placed in a class inferior to their own. Teach them by word and example to respect old age and never to mock and joke about the defects which old age causes physically or mentally.

Teach them to love all mankind, without distinction of caste. Teach them that one must be always ready to assist those who are in need of help and never to be afraid of spending time and money on them. That they must, in a word, always think of others rather than of themselves, and that, in acting thus one feels an inner satisfaction for which the egoist always looks in vain.

Develop self-confidence in them. Have them understand that before embarking on any enterprise or business venture, it should be thoroughly analysed by critical reasoning, avoiding impulsiveness; and once they have arrived at a decision they should stick to it, unless some additional facts prove that they had been mistaken.

Teach them above all that they must set out in life with the very definite idea that they will succeed! Under the influence of this idea they inevitably will succeed, not by sitting down quietly expecting events to happen, but influenced by this idea they will do all that is necessary for complete success. They will know how to profit by opportunities and, if there should be but one single opportunity coming their way, will seize it, even if it were by a single thread; while he who distrusts himself may be likened to Constant Guignard, who never succeeds in anything because he does exactly all that prevents success. Such a one might swim in a perfect ocean of opportunities, all with heads of hair like Absalom himself, but would neither see them, nor seize even a single one. Such a one often creates for himself the very circumstances which cause failure, while he who is saturated with the idea of success unconsciously creates favorable circumstances which carry him along to the summit.

Parents and teachers should make it a point to instruct by example. The child is impressionable and open to suggestion. What he sees being done, he will want to do also. Parents should therefore, be very careful to set only good examples for their children.

"Suggestions"—by Parents

To overcome faults and defects in children and to develop good habits and desirable qualities, the following suggestion will prove a powerful aid.

Parents should wait until the child is in bed, and asleep; then father or mother should noiselessly enter the room, approach the bed, within a yard, and murmur to the child fifteen or twenty times over, all the things you wish the child to do or to be as regards health, sleep, work, application, conduct, etc.; then retire as noiselessly as you came, taking great care not to awaken the child. This extremely simple proceeding always gives most satisfactory results, and it is easy to understand the reason why it should. When the child sleeps, his body and his conscious being are at rest; his *Unconscious self,* however, is awake. You speak therefore, to the *latter alone* and as it is very credulous, it accepts what you say without contradiction and, little by little, the child becomes what the parents desire it to be.

Let fathers and mothers consider this as a sacred duty to their children. It is mental and moral food, as necessary to them as physical food.

"Suggestions"—by Teachers

It is very desirable that teachers should make suggestions to their pupils every morning, somewhat in this manner:

"My friends, I expect you to be always polite and kind to everybody and obedient to your parents and teachers. Whenever they give you an order, or tell you something, you will always listen attentively and obey the order or instructions given you in a cheerful manner. Never look upon it as an irksome, or tiresome task. Hitherto you may have thought, once in a while, that the order was merely given to annoy you, but now you understand very well that it is in your own interest and for your own good that things are being told and explained to you. Therefore, instead of being cross and disagreeable, you will now be thankful to your elders.

"Furthermore, you will now love your work, whatever it may be. At present it will chiefly consist of study. In your lessons you will always enjoy the things you are to study, even those for which hitherto you had no inclination.

"When a teacher is giving you a lesson, in class or otherwise, you will devote all your attention, exclusively and solely, to what he says, without occupying your mind in any way with the silly or stupid things which your companions may have said or done; and especially without doing or saying anything of the kind yourselves.

"Under such conditions, as you *are* intelligent, and you are intelligent, my friends, you will easily understand and remember your lessons. What you have learned will be stowed away in the pigeonholes of your memory, where it remains at your disposal and where you can take it out for use, whenever you have need or use for it.

"Likewise when you are alone, working at your lessons at home, or busy at a task, you will fix your attention solely on the work in hand. In this way you will always obtain good marks for your lessons."

This method, if truly and faithfully followed, will produce a race endowed with the highest physical and moral qualities.

Instructions for Practitioners of the "Method"

How To Teach People To Make Autosuggestions: Advice And Instructions To His Pupils And Disciples

By Emile Coué.

Instructions in the method of inducing *good auto-suggestions* by the sick and afflicted are brief, but are sufficient if followed.

The principle of the method may be summed up in these few words:

IT IS IMPOSSIBLE TO THINK OF TWO THINGS AT THE SAME TIME: That is to say, two ideas may be in *juxtaposition*, but they cannot be superimposed in our mind.

EVERY THOUGHT THAT COMPLETELY FILLS OUR MIND BECOMES TRUE FOR US AND HAS A TENDENCY TO TRANSFORM ITSELF INTO ACTION.

Therefore, if you can cause a sick person to *think* that his or her trouble is getting better, *it will disappear*. If you are able to make a kleptomaniac *think* that he will not steal any more, he will stop stealing—he is cured.

Always encourage your patients; try to arouse in them friendly sentiments and absolute confidence. You will be aided in your experiments by their willing obedience. If you induce a mental attitude of satisfaction and good will the desired results will be gotten more easily.

Praise is a stimulus, but not when it is exaggerated. Reproach is also a stimulus, but it hurts and, if continued, rankles deeply. I use words which do not wound, embodying needed reproaches in light phrases which no one can properly object to, and which they do not object to because they feel that I do not mean only to reproach. You may reproach yourself, but if another reproaches you, it irritates. I do not make reproaches, *I state facts.*

You must have absolute confidence that you are going to do some good to every patient you treat. Assure yourself that you are able to do your part, not passably but efficiently, provided it is reasonable.

Let the very tone of your voice convey your assurance. Be unaffected in manner and plain in speech; but, at the same time, be very firm, almost commanding, with a patient.

Always use a commanding tone which permits of no disobedience. I do not say that it is necessary to raise the voice; it is, on the contrary, preferable to speak in the ordinary pitch, but to lay stress on each syllable in crisp, decisive tones.

Should a patient be cold and unsympathetic at first, do not let that trouble you, or hinder you from following your usual method of treatment. On the contrary *double and treble* your efforts. Say to yourself: "Although he is cold and unsympathetic now, he is going to like me and become friendly." Then the patient's attitude will not affect you; it will change into friendliness.

Training, with such results, may seem impossible to you, yet it is the simplest thing in the world. All that is necessary is to teach the patient, by a series of appropriate and graduated experiments, the A B C of *conscious autosuggestion*.

Here is the series. If you follow it to the letter you may be sure, absolutely sure, of obtaining good results, excepting with the two types of people previously mentioned.

First Experiment
(Preparatory)

Ask the patient to stand upright, with body stiff as an iron bar, feet close together from heel to toe, but with the ankles flexible, as if they were hinges. Tell him to think of himself as of a post, hinged at its base, nicely balanced on the floor. Remind him that pushing the post slightly, either forward or backward, will tumble it to the floor without the least resistance, whichever way it is pushed. Say that you are going to pull him back by the shoulders and that he is to allow himself to fall straight into your arms, *without the slightest resistance*, turning on his ankles as a post would on hinges; that is to say, keeping his feet on the floor. Next pull him back by the shoulders and if the experiment does not succeed at once, repeat until it does, or practically so.

Second Experiment

Explain to the patient that in order to show him the action of imagination on ourselves, you are going to ask him in a moment to think: "I am falling backward, etc.," that he must not have any other thought in mind, that he must not reflect for a moment as to whether he is going to fall or not, or think that in falling he might hurt himself, etc. . . . that he must not, in order to please you, try to fall backward purposely, but that on the other hand if he really feels an indefinable something that impels him, he *must not resist* but *must obey* that impulse. Then ask him to hold his head high and to shut his eyes. Place your right fist on the back of his neck and the left hand on his forehead, and tell him: THINK: *"I'm falling backward . . . I'm falling backward"* . . . *and "you will fall backward, you . . . fall . . . back . . . ward . . . ,* etc." At the same time move your left hand lightly backward on his left temple above the ear and slowly, very slowly, but with a continuous movement, withdraw the right fist. The patient will make a movement backward and either stop himself from falling or fall down completely. In the first case tell him that he has resisted; that he did not have in his mind only the thought of falling, but also the thought that he would hurt himself if he did fall. And that is true, for if he did not have that thought he would have fallen plump to the floor. Repeat the experiment; speak in a commanding manner as if you would compel the patient to obey you. Continue in this way until you succeed completely, or practically so. I suggest that you stand at a little distance behind the patient, with your left leg forward and right leg well back, in order that you may not be knocked off your feet when he falls. If you neglect that precaution a double fall may happen, if the patient be a heavy person.

Third Experiment

Let the patient stand facing you, with body stiff, ankles flexible, feet together and parallel. Put both your hands on his temples without pressure; look at him fixedly, not moving your eyelids, but staring at the root of his nose; then tell him to think: *"I am falling forward, I am falling forward"* and repeat to him accentuating the syllables, *"You are . . . fall . . . ing . . . for . . . ward . . . You . . . are . . . fall . . . ing . . . forward*, etc.," never ceasing to look fixedly at him.

Fourth Experiment

Request the patient to clasp his hands and to press the fingers together as tightly as possible, that is to say until the fingers begin to tremble slightly; look at him fixedly as in previous experiments, and keep your hands on his, pressing the latter slightly as though you wanted to press them together more tightly. Tell him to think that he is unable to unclasp his fingers; that you are going to count to three, and when you say THREE he should try to separate his hands while thinking only: *"I cannot do it . . . I cannot . . . , etc.,"* and he will find that he is unable to do it. Count: *one . . . two . . . three . . .* very slowly and add at once: "*You . . . can . . . not . . . do . . . it.*" "*You . . . can . . . not . . . do . . . it.*" If the patient thinks solely: "*I cannot do it,*" he will not only be unable to unclasp his fingers but the fingers will press themselves all the harder together—the greater his efforts to separate them. The effect is exactly contrary to what he tries to do. After a few seconds tell him "Now think: *I can,*" and his fingers will unclasp of themselves.

It is essential that you should keep your eyes fixed at the root of his nose, and do not allow the patient to turn his eyes away from yours for a single moment. If he should be able to separate his hands while you say: "*You . . . can . . . not,*" do not think that it is YOUR fault; it is that of the subject who has *not been thinking solely*: "I CANNOT." Tell him so in a decided manner, and try the experiment over again.

When these experiments have succeeded, all others will succeed equally well. Results will be easily gotten by following, to the letter, the instructions given.

Use no unnecessary words and encourage none. Just say: "You suffer from neurasthenia. I know better than you do what ails you and how much you suffer (it always satisfies them to be told that they suffer), and I also know that you are going to get rid of your ailment."

Never *pity* a patient. They may say: "Oh! You have a heart of stone." You reply: "It is in your own interest; if I were to pity you, I would be doing you a bad turn."

I purposely employ terms which are not vulgar, but familiar ones; they are more forceful.

Speak in a calm voice, as one who is accustomed to be obeyed.

The voice is what we make it. It is susceptible of cultivation. Therefore cultivate your voice. Whoever will take a little trouble, *can acquire* a good one.

The further I go the more I see that one must not even *force attention*. By observation, I try to imitate nature. The shorter and simpler the instruction the better it is. Do not try to make several suggestions at a time. "EVERY DAY, IN EVERY WAY, I AM GETTING BETTER AND BETTER," answers for everything. One person had been unable to open his hand for years, notwithstanding treatment by many physicians. Dr. Vachet made him open that hand instantly by putting into his mind the thought "*I can.*"

Some patients yield far more readily than others. It is easy to recognise such by the ready way in which their fingers and limbs contract—almost at once. After two or three successful experiments it is no longer necessary to tell them: "Think this," or "think that." You simply tell them, for instance, but in the firm imperative tone used by all good suggestionists: *"Close your hands. Now you cannot open them." "Close your eyes. Now you cannot open them, etc.,"* and you will see that the patient will find it absolutely impossible to open either hands or eyes, in spite of his very best efforts. After a few moments tell him: *"You can,"* and instantly the contraction will cease.

Experiments may be varied infinitely. Here are a few more:

- Let the patient join his hands and suggest to him that they are welded together:
- Place his hand on the table and suggest that it is stuck to it:
- Tell him that he is fixed to his chair, and that he cannot rise from it:
- Make him rise and tell him that it is impossible for him to walk:
- Put a penholder on the table and tell him that it weighs 100 kilos and he is unable to lift it, etc. etc.

In all these experiments I cannot lay too much stress on the fact that it is not *suggestion*, properly speaking, which produces the phenomena, but *autosuggestion*, which is produced in the patient by the *suggestion* of the practitioner.

Curative Suggestion Methods

When the patient has passed through the preliminary experiments and has understood them, he is prepared for curative suggestion, like a cultivated field in which seed may germinate and develop; before that he was like unplowed ground on which seed would perish.

Whatever the ailment of the patient may be, physical or mental, it is important to *proceed always in the same way* and to *use the same words* with few variations, according to the case. You say to the patient:

"Sit down and close your eyes:

"I will not try to put you to sleep; it is not necessary:

"I request you to close your eyes, simply for the purpose that your attention may not be distracted by the things you see around you:

"Now impress upon your mind that every word I say is going to fix itself in your brain and be firmly imprinted, engraved, embedded there:

"My words will always stay there fixed, imprinted, embedded, and without your will or knowledge, in fact wholly unconsciously on your part, you yourself and your entire organism are going to obey:

"I tell you, first of all, that every day, three times a day, at morning, noon and evening, at the usual meal hours, you will be hungry, that is to say: you will feel the pleasing sensation that makes you think: 'Oh! I am ready to eat with great satisfaction':

"You will indeed eat with great pleasure and enjoy your food, of course without over-eating; you will be careful to chew your food thoroughly so as to transform it into a sort of soft paste which you will then swallow:

"Your food will be properly digested and you will not feel the slightest discomfort, inconvenience, or pain—neither in the stomach nor in the intestines:

"You will assimilate your food well and your organism will profit by it in making blood, muscle, strength, energy—in a word: LIFE.

"Having digested properly, the function of excretion will be perfectly normal:

"Every morning, on rising, you will feel a desire for an evacuation; without ever requiring medicine or artificial means of any kind, you will obtain entirely normal and satisfactory bowel movements.

"Furthermore, every night, from the moment you wish to sleep to the time at which you desire to awake in the morning, you will sleep a profound, calm, wholesome, unbroken sleep, during which you will have no nightmares; upon waking you will feel well, cheerful, and ready for active work.

"If at times you have been sad and depressed; if you have been brooding and worrying, this will cease from now on, and instead of being sad, depressed and worried, you will feel cheerful, very cheerful, even gay; you may have no cause for your gaiety, just as you may have had no reason for your depression. Moreover I say that even if you have had any real reason for being sad or depressed, you are NOT going to be so.

"If it happens, sometimes, that you have fits of impatience and ill temper, you will never have them again. On the contrary you will always be patient; always *master of yourself*; and the things which worried, irritated and annoyed you will henceforth leave you absolutely indifferent and perfectly calm.

"If you are at times attacked, pursued, haunted by bad and unwholesome ideas, by apprehensions, fears, aversions, temptations, or grudges against others, all will gradually disappear from your mind; they will fade away and be lost as in a passing cloud, and will finally disappear completely; as a dream vanishes on awakening, so will all your vain imaginations vanish.

"I say that all your organs are performing their functions properly:

"The heart beats normally, the circulation of the blood is as it should be:

"The lungs are in fine condition:

"The stomach, the intestines, the liver, the bladder, the kidneys and the biliary duct are all functioning properly:

"If at this moment one of them should not be acting normally, this abnormality will be less day by day and very soon it will have vanished completely and the organ will be in perfect working order.

"Further, if there should be any lesions in any one of these organs they will improve day by day and soon be entirely healed.*

"I must also add, and it is of extreme importance, that if up to the present, you have lacked confidence in yourself, I tell you that distrust in yourself will gradually disappear and give place to *self-confidence*, based on your knowledge of that force of incalculable power which is in you.

"This self-confidence is absolutely necessary for you and every other human being to have. *Without it* you will never get anywhere; *with it*, you may accomplish whatever you want to (within the laws of nature, of course).

---

* In this connection I will say that it is not necessary to know which organ is afflicted in order to heal it. Under the influence of the autosuggestion *"Every day, in every way, I am getting better and better"* the *Unconscious* exercises its influence on the particular, diseased organ.

"You are now going to have confidence in yourself and this confidence enables you to believe that you can reach each goal you set for yourself (if it is a natural one):

"And that you will do well all that, in the course of duty, you have to do.

"So then, when you wish to do something that is natural, or when you have a duty to perform, always think that it is an easy thing to do. The words: *'It is difficult, impossible, I cannot, it is beyond me, I cannot help myself. . .'* must disappear entirely from your vocabulary. Think: 'IT IS EASY . . . I CAN.' Believing a matter to be easy, *it becomes so* for you, although it may seem difficult to others. You will do it quickly and well, without fatigue, because you do it without effort."

All *suggestions* must be made in a monotonous, soothing voice (emphasizing, however, the essential words) which causes the patient, though not to actually sleep, yet to become somewhat drowsy and stop thinking of anything, thus permitting your words to penetrate more deeply into his *unconscious self.*

To these general suggestions, which may seem rather lengthy and even childish to some, but still are NECESSARY, add others that apply to the particular case of the patient you have under your care.

When you have finished your series of suggestions you say to the patient:

"In short, I mean that from every point of view, physical and mental, you are going to enjoy excellent health, better health than you have been able to enjoy hitherto:

"I am now going to count three, and when I say 'THREE'

you will open your eyes and come out of the passive state in which you are now:

"You will come out of it very quietly, without feeling in the least drowsy or tired:

"On the contrary you will feel strong, vigorous, alert, active, full of life:

"Moreover you will be cheerful, fit and well in every respect:

"ONE . . . TWO . . . THREE . . ."

At the word "three" the patient opens his eyes, always with a smile and an expression of well-being and contentment on his face. Sometimes, although rarely, the patient is cured instantly. At other times, and more generally, the patient feels relieved, his pain or ailment disappears partially or totally, but for a time only.

In most cases it is necessary to repeat the *suggestions* more or less frequently, but at longer and longer intervals according to the progress made by your patient, until they become unnecessary; that is, when the cure is complete.

Before dismissing your patient, impress upon him that he carries *within himself* the instrument of self-cure; that you are, so to speak, only an instructor, teaching him how to use this instrument, and that he must constantly help you to help him. Therefore, every morning before rising and every night as soon as he is in bed, he must close his eyes and mentally transport himself into your presence, and then repeat twenty times in a monotonous tone, using a string with 20 knots for counting, this phrase:

> ### "Every Day, in Every Way,
> ### I am Getting Better and Better."

Mentally, he must underline the words, IN EVERY WAY which apply to everything, mental or physical.

This *general suggestion* is more effective than *special suggestions*.

The Superiority of this Method

This method has given absolutely marvelous results and it is easy to understand the reason why. Indeed, if you follow closely my advice, it becomes impossible for you to fail (excepting of course with the two classes of people before mentioned, who fortunately represent barely 3% of the mass).

On the other hand, if you try to put your patients to sleep right away, without explanations and preliminary experiments, which are necessary to get them to accept your *suggestions* and so transform them into *autosuggestions*, you cannot and will not succeed; excepting perhaps in cases of extraordinarily sensitive people, and there are not many such.

Everyone may become responsive by training, but *very few are so* without that preliminary instruction which I have recommended, and which can be given in a few minutes.

Formerly I labored under the impression that *suggestions* could only be given while the patient was asleep, and so I always tried to induce sleep; but finding that it was not indispensable, I ceased doing it to spare patients that feeling of fear and uneasiness, which they usually have when told that he or she is going to be put to sleep. That fear often induces *involuntary resistance* against sleep. If, on the contrary, you tell a patient that you are not going to put him to sleep, you immediately gain his confidence, and he listens with a receptive mind free from disturbance or opposition. It often happens, that, soothed by the monotonous sound of your voice, the patient falls soundly asleep and wakes up astonished at having been asleep.

If there are skeptics amongst you, and there are sure to be some, I say to you simply this: "Come to my house, see what is being done there and be convinced by the facts."

Do not think, however, that it is absolutely necessary to proceed exactly and only in the way I have indicated in order to make *suggestions* and bring about *autosuggestions*. It is possible to make suggestions to some people without their knowing it and without any preparation at all. For instance, if a physician, who by his title alone has already a suggestive influence on his patient, were to tell him that he can do nothing for him, that his illness is incurable, he would induce in the mind of the patient an *autosuggestion* which might have the most disastrous consequences. If, on the other hand, the physician tells the patient that, although his illness is a serious one, with time, care, and patience he will certainly be cured, he often obtains results that are surprising.

The influence of the mind upon the body exists undeniably and is infinitely greater than is commonly supposed. It is immense, immeasurable. It often causes contractions or paralyses which may be only temporary, but which may also last through life, unless something extraordinary occurs to change the mental and therefore the physical state of the patient.

Make up your mind that you are going to obtain certain results and you will find the *ways and means*; that is the apparently strange part of it. If you consider it your duty to take folks to the clinics, you will find words to induce them to go and even to cause them to *desire to go*.

It is easy to understand the part played by the one who gives the *suggestions*. It is not a *Master* who commands; he is a friend, a *guide* who helps the patient step by step along the path of recovery. As all the *suggestions* are given in the interest of the patient the *Unconscious* of the latter is perfectly content to assimilate them and transform them into *autosuggestions*. When this is done, a cure follows more or less rapidly.

Another example: Suppose a physician, after examining his patient, were to write out a prescription and hand it over without a word of comment; the prescribed remedies will not have much effect. But if he explains to his patient that such and such medicines must be taken in such and such conditions and that they will produce certain results, it is practically certain that the expected results will be brought about.

If there are medical men or brother chemists in my audience, I trust they will not look upon me as their enemy; I am, on the contrary, their best friend. On the one hand I would like to inscribe on the curricula of medical schools the study of theoretical and practical *suggestion* for the benefit of the sick, and of the physicians themselves; also, it is my opinion that when a patient visits his physician, the latter should *always* prescribe one or more remedies, even if not necessary. It is a fact that when a patient goes to see his physician, it is to ask what remedy will cure him. He does not know that, in most cases, it is the hygiene and regimen which do this, so he attaches little importance to them. What he wants is medicine.

In my opinion, if the physician prescribes a diet only, without medicine, his patient will be satisfied. He will say that it was not worth while seeing his physician without having anything prescribed for him, and often goes to another. It seems to me that a physician should always prescribe medicine for his patient and, as much as possible, medicines made up by himself, rather than the advertised remedies which owe their value to advertisements only. His own prescription will inspire infinitely more confidence than the *pills* or *powders* of *So* and *So* which anyone can obtain in the nearest drug store, without the need of a prescription.

What Autosuggestion Has Done

Observations of Some Remarkable Cures

By Emile Coué.

This little monograph would be incomplete if it did not include a few typical examples of the actual cures ejected. The whole list would be too long, and it might prove tiresome if I were to mention all the cases which I have treated. I will therefore, content myself with citing a few of the more remarkable ones.

In order to show that these cures are permanent, I have purposely chosen some cases of older dates, as well as a few of the more recent ones.

Tuberculosis.

Mrs. D., of Troyes, about 30 years of age, in the last stages of consumption; grew thinner and thinner daily in spite of special feeding. There was coughing, spitting, oppression and difficulty in breathing; indeed from all appearances she had only a few months more to live; preliminary experiments show great sensitiveness and *suggestion* is followed by immediate improvement; from the very next day the morbid symptoms began to be less pronounced; the improvement became more marked daily, and the weight of the patient increased rapidly although she no longer took specially nourishing foods; after a few months the cure was apparently complete. This lady wrote me on the 1st of January, 1911 (that was 8 months after I had left Troyes), a letter of thanks, informing me that although pregnant, she was perfectly well.

Miss X., of Geneve, 13 years of age, has a sore on the temple which several doctors considered to be of tubercular origin and various treatments extending over a period of a year and a half had availed nothing; she was then taken to Mr. Baudouin, a disciple of Mr. Coué, residing at Geneva; was treated by suggestion and told to return in a week; when she came back the sore was healed!

Congestion of the Lungs.

Mrs. Z., of Nancy, in January 1919, contracted congestion of the lungs, from which she had not recovered after two months; there was general weakness, loss of appetite, indigestion, rare and difficult bowel action, insomnia, and copious night-sweats; after the. very first treatment the patient felt much better; two days later she came to tell me that she was perfectly well; every trace of illness had disappeared and every organ functioned normally; three or four times she had been on the verge of having night-sweats again, but each time prevented it by conscious *autosuggestions*. From that time on, Mrs. Z. has enjoyed perfect health.

Asthma.

Miss M. D., of Troyes, suffered for eight years from asthma which compelled her to sit up in bed nearly all night, struggling for breath, when her respiratory organs failed to function; preliminary experiments showed her to be a very sensitive subject, going to sleep immediately the suggestion is given. Results: from the very first day there is great improvement; the patient passed a good night, interrupted by only a single attack of asthma, which lasted but a quarter of an hour; in a very short time the asthma disappeared completely, and without recurrence thereafter.

Bronchitis.

Mr. Hazel, 48 years, of Brin, taken ill the 15th of January, 1915, with chronic bronchitis, growing worse daily; he came to me in October 1915; there was an immediate improvement which has been maintained ever since. At the time of writing he is not completely cured but is very much better.

Senility of Larynx.

Mr. X., a Professor of Belfort, could not talk for more than ten or fifteen minutes without his throat becoming very irritated; various doctors told him that there was no lesion in the vocal organs, but one stated that there was senility of the larynx, which led him to believe that he could never be cured; he came to Nancy for a vacation, and a lady friend advised him to see me. He refused, at first, but finally consented in spite of his absolute disbelief in the effects of suggestion; I treated him, notwithstanding, and requested him to come back in a couple of days; he came and told me that on the previous day he had been able to converse all afternoon without the slightest indication of his old trouble; two days later he came to see me again, to say that he had been absolutely free from sore throat although he had not only been talking all the time, but also had been bold enough to sing the previous evening. The cure still holds good and I am convinced that it is a lasting one.

Pott's Disease.

Mr. Nagengast, aged 18, rue Sellier No. 39, suffering from Pott's disease. He came to me early in 1914, having been encased in a plaster corset for six months. He came twice a week to the regular sittings and himself made the usual *autosuggestion*, mornings and evenings. The improvement manifested itself very rapidly and very soon the patient was able to do without his plaster-corset. I saw him again in 1916. He was entirely cured, carrying on his duties as a postman, after having been an "Infirmier," tending the sick in connection with the Nancy ambulance service where he had stayed until the service had been discontinued.

Eczema.

Mrs. H., of Maxeville, suffers from eczema, particularly intense on the left leg; both legs swollen and inflamed, especially at the ankles; walking difficult and painful; *suggestions*: the same evening Mrs. H. was able to walk several hundred yards without fatigue; the next morning the feet and ankles were no longer swollen and have not been swollen since; the eczema disappeared rapidly.

Gout.

Mr. E., of Troyes, had an attack of gout; the right ankle was inflamed and painful and he was unable to walk; the preliminary experiments proved him to be a very responsive subject; after the first treatment he was able to walk to the carriage which brought him, without using his cane for support; there was no more pain; the next day he did not come back, as I had instructed him to do; later his wife came to tell me that her husband had risen early that morning, had put on his shoes, and gone off on a bicycle to his workshop (he is a painter). Just imagine my astonishment. I have not been able to follow up this case as the patient never troubled himself to come and see me again. I learned later that he had gone a long time without any relapse, but I do not know what has become of him.

Club Feet.

T. Maurice, 8½ years old, of Nancy, has club feet. A first operation cured the left foot (or nearly so), the right foot remaining crippled. Two subsequent operations did no good.

The child was brought to me for the first time in February 1915. He walked fairly well, owing to two contrivances which held his feet straight. An improvement was noticed immediately after the first treatment, and after the second the child was able to walk in ordinary shoes. On April 17th the child was quite well. The right foot, however, is not quite as strong as it was, because of a sprain which was received on February 20th, 1916.

Rheumatism.

Mrs. Meder, 52 years, of Einville. For six months she suffered from pain in the right knee, accompanied by swelling which made the bending of the knee impossible. She saw me, for the first time, on 7th December 1917. She came again, on 4th of January 1918, to tell me that she suffered no more pain and that she was able to walk quite normally.

Mr. Ferry Eugene, 60 years, rue de la Cote 56, had rheumatic pains in the shoulder and the left leg for five years. He walked with difficulty leaning on a cane and could not lift his arms above the shoulder. He consulted me on 17th of September 1917. After the first visit the pains had entirely vanished and the patient could not only take long strides but could also run. Moreover he could whirl his arms like a windmill. I saw him again in November and there had been no relapse.

Mrs. Castelli, 41 years, of Einville (M-et-M) for thirteen years intermittent rheumatic pain in the right knee. Five years ago she had a more violent attack than ever before: the knee as well as the leg began swelling considerably and then the lower part of the leg atrophied and the patient was reduced to walking very painfully with the aid of a cane or a crutch. I saw her for the first time on 5th of November 1917 and she walked away without the help of either cane or crutch. Since then she never had any more use for the crutch but occasionally did use the cane. Once in a while the pain in the knee recurs but is very slight.

Palsy.

Mr. X., post-office clerk at Luneville, lost a child in January 1910; this caused a cerebral disturbance which manifested itself by uncontrollable nervous trembling; his uncle brought him to me in the month of June; preliminary experiments were followed by *suggestions*; four days later he came back to tell me that his trembling had disappeared; I repeated the *suggestions*, with instructions to call again in a week; the week went by, then two, three, four weeks passed with no news from him; a little while afterwards his uncle came to tell me that he had received a letter from his nephew, informing him that the latter was perfectly well; that he had been re-instated in his position as telegraph-clerk—which he had previously been obliged to abandon—and that on the day he wrote the letter, he had sent off a lengthy telegram of 170 words, without the least difficulty; he added in his letter that he could have easily sent off an even longer one. There has been no relapse.

Stammering.

Miss Linier, 15 years, rue Montet 88, stammered from infancy. She came on July 20, 1917, and was instantly delivered from her defect. I saw her a month later and found her permanently cured.

Kidney Disease.

Mrs. P., of Laneuveville, had pains in her kidneys and knees; her complaint dated back 10 years; she was going from bad to worse every day. *Suggestion*, on my part and *autosuggestion*, on her part; improvement was immediate and progressed satisfactorily. She was rapidly and permanently cured.

Enteritis.

Mr. A. G., of Troyes, has suffered for a long time from enteritis (inflammation of the bowels) which different treatments failed to cure; he was in a very bad way, being depressed, gloomy, unsociable and obsessed by thoughts of suicide; preliminary experiments being satisfactory, *suggestion* followed; appreciable results showed from the very first day; continued suggestions for three months, at first daily, then at increasingly longer intervals; at the end of that time, there was a complete cure; the enteritis had entirely disappeared and his mental condition was excellent. As this cure dates back for twelve years, without the slightest relapse, it may well be considered to be permanent.

Mr. G. is a striking example of the effects that can be produced by suggestion, or rather by *autosuggestion*. While I was making suggestions from the physical point of view, I also did so from a mental point of view and he accepted the one suggestion as well as the other. His self-confidence increased daily and, as he was an excellent workman, in order to earn more, he tried to obtain a machine which would enable him to work at home. Some time afterwards a manufacturer, who had seen with his own eyes how good a workman he was, entrusted him with the very machine he so much desired. Thanks to his skill Mr. G. was able to turn out more work than an ordinary worker. Delighted with the result, his employer gave him another and still another machine until Mr. G., who, but for his recourse to *suggestions* would have remained an ordinary workman, now is in charge of six machines which net him a handsome income.

Nervous Dyspepsia.

Mrs. T., of Nancy, had neurasthenia, dyspepsia, gastralgia, enteritis, and pains in different parts of the body; she treated herself for several years with negative results; I gave her *suggestions* which she turned into *auto-suggestions*, daily. There was a noticeable improvement, from the first day, which continued without interruption; she was cured long ago, both mentally and physically; she follows no special diet; thinks there still is, perhaps, a slight touch of enteritis but is not sure.

Neuralgia.

Mrs. L., of Nancy; pains in the right side of the face, over a period of more than 10 years; consulted many physicians whose prescriptions did not help; finally an operation was decided upon, but, first, she came to me on the 25th of July, 1916; her improvement was immediate; after 10 days the pain vanished and, up to December 20th, there was no recurrence.

Mrs. Lacour, 63 years, Chemin des Sables, had pains in the face for the past ten years. All treatments taken tad availed her nothing and when an operation was advised, she refused to submit to it. She consulted me for the first time on 25th of July 1916. Four days later the pains had vanished and she never had them again up to this day.

Neurasthenia.

Mr. Y., of Nancy, a sufferer from neurasthenia for several years, has aversions, nervous fears, disorders of the stomach and intestines; his sleep is broken, he is gloomy and haunted by ideas of suicide; when walking he staggers like a drunken man and can think of nothing but his trouble; all other methods had failed and he went from bad to worse; a month's treatment in a sanitarium had not the slightest effect. Mr. Y. came to see me early in October, 1910; the preliminary experiments proved comparatively easy; I explained to the patient the principles of *autosuggestion*, and also the existence within us of the *conscious* and the *unconscious being*; then I made suggestions; for two or three days Mr. Y. had a little trouble in grasping the explanations which I had given him, but in a little while his clouded mind saw the light, and he understood; I gave him fresh suggestions and he transformed them into *autosuggestions* every day adding others, of his own accord; the improvement was slow at first, but, little by little it progressed more rapidly; in a month and a half the cure was complete. The ex-invalid who so recently had looked upon himself as a most miserable man, now considers himself most happy. Not only has there been no relapse but it is impossible for such to occur, because Mr. Y. is firmly convinced that he could not fall back into his former miserable state of existence.

Mrs. X., a sister of Mrs. T., had a very bad case of neurasthenia and remained in bed two weeks out of every four; it was impossible for her to move or work; suffered from lack of appetite, depression, and digestive disorders. She was cured in one single sitting and the cure seems to be a lasting one, as she has never had a relapse.

Miss D., of Mirecourt, 16 years old, suffered for the past three years from nervous attacks. These attacks, infrequent in the beginning, kept recurring at shorter intervals. When she came to me on April 1st, 1917, she had had three attacks in two weeks. From that time to April 18th there was not a single attack. I may add that since taking the treatment, this young girl was no longer troubled with bad headaches from which she had previously suffered almost constantly.

Varicose Ulcers.

Mrs. Urbain Marie, aged 55, of Maxeville had been suffering from varicose ulcers for a year and a half. The first treatment took place in September 1915, the second treatment a week later. There was an absolute cure in two weeks.

Mrs. H., rue Guilbert-de-Pixérécourt, Nancy, 49 years old, varicose ulcer since September 1914 which was treated by her Doctor without success. The lower part of the leg was greatly enlarged. The ulcer was as large as a two Francs piece, was located above the ankle and went to the bone. The inflammation was very intense, the suppuration was abundant and the pain extremely violent. The patient called for the first time in April 1916. An improvement was noticeable after the first visit and continued without interruption. By the 18th of February the swelling had gone down *completely* and the pain and irritation had vanished. The sore was still there, but it was no larger than a pea and only 2 or 3 millimeters in depth. It still discharged very slightly. In 1920 the cure had long been complete.

Mr. Philippe Schirer, 48 years, of Bouxieres-aux-Dames, came for the first time on 20th of April 1917, with a 15 year old varicose sore on the left leg, as large as a five Francs piece. On the 27th of April the sore was healed. Saw him again on 4th of May and found the cure to be permanent.

Ulcer.

Miss X., of Blainville, had a sore on the left foot, probably of specific origin. A slight sprain caused a swelling of the foot, accompanied by acute pains. Various treatments had done no good and after a little while a suppurating sore appeared which seemed to indicate caries of the bone. Walking became more and more difficult in spite of continuous treatments. On the advice of a former patient of mine, she came to me and relief was noticeable after the first few visits. Gradually the swelling went down, the pain became less intense, the suppuration became less and less and finally the sore was healed completely. It took a few months to get this result. At this writing the foot is almost normal and although the pain and swelling have disappeared, the backward flexion of the foot is not yet perfect, which causes the patient to limp slightly.

Abscess.

Miss Z., also of Geneva, had undergone an operation for an abscess above the knee when she was 17 years old and had, as a consequence, a drawn-up right leg. She requested Mr. Baudouin to give a treatment by suggestion and he had hardly commenced doing so, when the leg began to bend back and forth in a normal manner. (It must be admitted that there was a psychological cause in this case.)

Frontal Sinus.

Mr. B. had suffered for 24 years from inflammation of the frontal cavity (sinus) which had been operated upon 11 times. But in spite of all that had been done the inflammation (sinusite) persisted, causing intolerable pains. The physical state of the patient was extremely pitiable. He had almost continuously violent pains, no appetite, extreme weakness and could neither walk, read, nor sleep. His nerves were in no better state than his body and notwithstanding the treatment of such men as Bernheim of Nancy, Dejerine of Paris, Dubois of Berne, X. of Strasbourg, this pitiable state continued and grew worse every day.

On the advice of one of my former patients, he came to me in September 1915. From that moment his health improved rapidly and at the present time (1921) he is *perfectly well*. This was a real resurrection.

Heart Disease.

Emile Chenu, 10 years old, of 19 Grande Rue (a refugee from Metz), had heart trouble of uncertain nature; bled from the mouth every night; his first visit was in July 1915; after a few treatments the loss of blood became less; improvement continued, and by the end of November he was completely cured. There has been no relapse since August 1916.

Young B., 13 years old, entered a hospital in January, 1912; had very serious heart trouble, characterized by difficulty in breathing; can walk only with very slow and short steps. The doctor who attended him was one of our best physicians and predicted a rapid and fatal issue.

The patient left the hospital in February, no better! A friend of the family brought him to me. The moment I saw him, I considered him a hopeless case. Nevertheless I let him go through the preliminary experiments, to which he responded surprisingly well. After having given him suggestion and instructing him to do the same for himself, I told him to come back in two days. When I saw him the second time, I noticed to my great surprise a most remarkable improvement in his respiration and in his walking. I repeated the suggestive treatment. He returned again a few days later. The improvement had continued, and so it was at each subsequent visit.

My little patient made such rapid progress that three weeks after I first saw him, he was able to go on foot with his mother up to the plateau of Villers. His breathing was free and almost normal. He walked without getting out of breath and could even go upstairs, something which it was impossible for him to do a short three weeks ago. The improvement continued steadily and very soon he surprised me by asking my permission to go to Carignan to see his grandmother. As he seemed well enough I advised him to do so. He went, keeping in touch with me regularly by mail. His health is getting better and better;

he has a good appetite, his digestion and assimilation are good, and the feeling of oppression has left him entirely. Now he not only walks like everybody else, but even runs and chases butterflies.

He came back in the month of October and I hardly recognized him. The bent and puny little fellow who went away in May last had become a fine, tall, erect boy, whose face was the very picture of health. He had added twelve centimeters to his height and 19 lbs. to his weight. From that time on he has lived a perfectly normal life, he runs up and down stairs, rides a bicycle, and plays football.

Paralysis.

Mr. D., of Jarville, had paralysis of the left upper eyelid. He went to the hospital where he received injections, as a result of which the patient was able to raise his eyelid, but the left eye was deflected outward for more than 45 degrees, and an operation appeared to be necessary. He came to my house and, thanks to *autosuggestion*, his eye was restored, little by little, to its normal position.

Mr. M., a hat-maker, living at Sainte-Savine, near Troyes, was paralyzed for two years, following an injury at the junction of the spinal column and the pelvis; the paralysis existed only in the lower limbs in which the circulation of the blood had practically ceased, making them swollen, congested and discolored; various treatments, including antisyphilitic, had been tried without result; preliminary experiments were successful; suggestions given by me were transformed into *autosuggestions* by the patient, for a week; after that time there was an almost imperceptible, but nevertheless appreciable movement of the left leg. Renewed the *suggestions*: a week later the improvement was notable; in another two weeks a more and more noticeable improvement took place together with a slow, but progressive, lessening of the swelling, and so on; eleven months afterwards, on the 1st of November, 1906, the patient went downstairs alone, and walked 1,000 yards; in the month of July, 1907, he went back to his factory where he has since worked continuously, without the least trace of paralysis.

Womb Trouble.

Mrs. Jousselin, 60 years old, rue des Dominicains 6, came to me on 20th July, 1917, complaining of a violent pain in the right leg and a considerable swelling of the entire limb. She could only drag herself along moaning with pain. After the treatment she could, to her great astonishment, walk normally without feeling the least pain. When she came again four days later, she said that she had had no pain in the interval and the swelling had subsided. This woman informed me that since coming to my house she had also been cured of white discharges and of inflammation of the womb from which she had suffered a long time. In November the cure was still holding good.

Mrs. Martin, Grande Rue (Ville Vieille) 105. Inflammation of the womb of thirteen years' standing, accompanied by pains and red and white discharges. The monthly periods were very painful and appeared every 22 or 23 days, lasting from ten to twelve days. First consultation on 15th of November 1917 and regular weekly visits thereafter. The patient felt better after the first treatment and improved rapidly until, in the beginning of January 1918, the inflammation had completely disappeared; her periods had become more regular and painless. A pain in the knee which the patient had also had for thirteen years, had disappeared likewise.

Mrs. M., 43 years, rue d'Amance 2, Malzéville, came toward the end of 1916 complaining of violent headaches which she has had almost all her life. After a few visits the pains had entirely disappeared.

About two months afterwards she noticed that she was also cured of a displacement of the womb, of which she had said nothing to me and to which she gaye no thought when making her *autosuggestions*. (This result is due to the words: "IN EVERY WAY," contained in the formula to be repeated mornings and evenings.)

Mrs. D., Choisy-le-Roi, had only one general suggestion on my part and thereafter made her autosuggestions morning and evening. In October of the same year this lady informed me that she was cured of a prolapsus of the womb which had troubled her for 20 years. Up to 1920 the cure is still permanent. (Same remark as in the preceding case.)

Metritis.

Mrs. E., of Chavigny, suffered from Metritis (inflammation of the womb) for 10 years. Came to me end of July
1916. There was an immediate improvement, the pain
and loss of blood diminished rapidly and by the 29th of
September both had disappeared The monthly period
which lasted from 8 to 10 days is now over in 4 days.

Thoughts and Precepts of Emile Coué

Recorded By Mme. Emile Leon.

———

"It is not the *person* who acts, it is the *method*."

"We can make, to ourselves, very much stronger suggestions than anyone else can, whoever that person may be."

"I do not impose anything on anybody. I simply help people *to do what they would like to do*, but what they believe themselves incapable of doing. It is not a contest but *an association* which exists between them and myself. It is not I that act, but a power *existing in themselves*, which I teach them to use."

"Contrary to general opinion, *autosuggestion is able to cure organic lesions*."

"Don't bother about the cause of an ailment; be concerned only about the effect, *and to make that effect disappear*, if such be at all natural."

"The words: *I would like to*, always imply: *But I cannot.* If you suffer, never say: 'I will *try* to get rid of this or that,' but say: *'I am going to cause it to disappear,'* for, if there is doubt, there is no result."

"The key to my METHOD is in the knowledge that the *imagination is superior to the will.* If both go together in the same direction, as in saying for instance: *'I will and I can,'* they are perfectly in accord; otherwise the *imagination always wins* over the *will.*"

"Many, who have taken medical treatments all their lives, expect to be cured at once by *autosuggestion.* That is a mistake. It is unreasonable to expect anything like that. It is useless to ask more of *autosuggestion* than what it can normally bring about, that is to say: a progressive improvement which slowly transforms itself into *complete recovery*, if the latter is at all natural."

"Develop the habit of expressing yourselves promptly, clearly, simply and with calm determination. Speak briefly, but distinctly—use no unnecessary words."

"Cultivate self-control. Avoid anger, for anger burns up our reserve energy; it *weakens* us. Anger never accomplishes anything good—only destroys. It is always an obstacle to success."

"Let us be calm, gentle, benevolent, sure of ourselves, and moreover let us be self-sufficient."

"The *Unconscious self* directs everything, both the physical and the moral. It presides over the functions of all the organs down to the infinitesimal cells of our system, through the intermediary of the nerves."

"To be afraid of becoming ill is to invite illness."

"It is an illusion to think that you have no illusions."

"Do not spend time trying to find maladies that you may possibly have; if you have no real ones, you are sure to create artificial ones."

"Man may be compared to a basin with a faucet at the top for filling, and a drain at the bottom (of larger diameter than the faucet) for emptying. If the drain be closed, the basin may be filled and kept full. When both vents are open at the same time, the basin is always empty. What happens, on the other hand, if the drain remains closed and the faucet open? The basin fills up and overflows.

"Now then, let us all keep our 'drains' closed, that is, let us not waste our strength. Let us make only one motion where no more are necessary, instead of twenty or forty motions as with some folks. Let us never act in great haste; and also think that what we have to do is easy, if it is at all possible of accomplishment. In this way our reservoir of strength will always be full, the inflow being more than sufficient for our ordinary needs, if we know how to use it economically."

"It's not the number of years that makes you old, but the *idea that you are getting old*. Many are still young at eighty, while others are old at forty."

"The altruist finds without seeking what the egoist seeks without finding."

"The more good you do *to others*, the more good you do *to yourself*."

"Rich is he who *thinks he is rich* and poor is he who *thinks he is poor*."

"He who possesses great wealth should use a large part of it to do good."

"When two people live together, the so-called *mutual concessions* usually come from the *same* person."

"Would you avoid ennui? Have several hobbies. When tired of one, play with another."

"Heredity shows itself mostly as a fatal realization of *the idea* of its existence."

"One who is born wealthy knows not the value of riches; he who always enjoys good health has no idea of the treasure he possesses.

"To appreciate riches, one must have known poverty. To appreciate good health, one must have been ill."

"It is better to be ignorant of evil and *avoid* it, than to be familiar with it and *cultivate* it."

"Simplify always—do not complicate."

"Stoics draw on *imagination* when, instead of saying: 'I *will not* suffer' they say: 'I *do not* suffer.'"

"One cannot have more than one idea in mind at a time; ideas follow one another without superimposing."

"If you practice conscious *autosuggestion*, do it in a natural way, quite simply, with firm conviction and especially without an effort. If *unconscious autosuggestions*, producing bad effects, manifest themselves so easily, it is just because they are made without any effort."

"Be absolutely certain, in your own mind, that you will get what you want, provided of course that you do not expect anything unnatural."

"To become *master of yourself* it is sufficient to *think that you are* master of yourself, or certainly going to be. If your hands tremble, if your steps are uncertain, tell yourself that all this is about to disappear and, little by little, it *will* disappear."

"It is not in *me* that you must have confidence, but in *yourself*; for in your *own self* is the power to heal. My part is simply to teach you how to use that power."

"Never discuss things you know nothing about, otherwise you will only say something foolish.

"Things that may seem extraordinary to you have a natural cause. If they appear extraordinary to your mind, it is because that cause has escaped you. Once you know the cause the thing appears to you as quite natural."

"It is the *imagination* and not the *will* which is the dominating faculty of man. It is a serious mistake to advise people to train their wills; they should learn to control and direct their *imaginations*."

"We do not see things as they are, but as they seem to be. This explains the contradictory evidence given by several eye-witnesses of an accident, though the statements of all are made in good faith."

"*Autosuggestion* is just one instrument which we must learn to use, like any other. The most perfect gun, in inexperienced hands, gives poor results; the more skilled your hands become, the more often you hit the bull's eye."

"*Conscious autosuggestion*, made with confidence, faith, and perseverance realizes itself automatically, in all matters within reason."

"If certain people do not obtain satisfactory results with *autosuggestion* it is because they lack confidence, or because they make efforts, the latter being more frequently the case. To make *good autosuggestions* it is absolutely necessary to make them *without effort*. The latter implies the use of the Will and that must be left out of the game entirely. You must have recourse *exclusively* to the *imagination*."

"The means employed by 'Healers' of all eras, have been based on *autosuggestion*, that is to say: their methods, of whatever kind—words, incantations, gestures, staging— have been designed to produce in the patient the *autosuggestion* of recovery and health."

"Every malady has a double aspect (unless it is exclusively a mental one). On every physical malady a mental one grafts itself. If we give to the physical illness the coefficient 1, the mental illness may have the coefficient 1, 2, 10, 20, 50, 100, or more. In many cases this mental coefficient may disappear instantly and if it was very high, 100 for instance, while that of the physical affection is 1, only the latter remains, that is 1/100th of the total illness. That would generally be considered a miracle; yet there is nothing miraculous about it."

"Contrary to common opinion physical diseases are, generally, more easily cured by *autosuggestion*, than mental ones."

"Buffon used to say: 'Fashion forms the man.' We would rather say: 'Man is what he thinks.' The fear of failure is almost certain to cause failure, just as the very idea of success brings success and enables one to overcome any obstacle in the way."

"It is as necessary for the practitioner of suggestion, as it is for the subject, to be convinced of results beforehand. It is this absolute conviction, this abundant faith, which enables him to obtain results, where all other means have failed."

"When you *believe* yourself to be master of your thoughts, you *become so*."

"Every thought, good or bad, becomes concrete; It materializes and becomes a reality, provided such is within the realm of possibility."

"We are that which *we make of ourselves*, not what *fate* makes us."

"Whoever starts in life with the thought firmly planted in his mind: '*I shall succeed*' always *does succeed* because he does what is necessary to that end. If an opportunity comes his way and if that opportunity has, so to speak, only one single hair on its head, he seizes it by that one hair. Moreover, he often brings about unconsciously or not, propitious circumstances. On the contrary, he who always doubts himself, will never arrive anywhere. Such a man might swim in an ocean full of opportunities with heads of hair like Absalom's. He would neither see nor seize a single one, even if he had only to reach out his hand and grasp it. Therefore, do not blame fate, blame *yourself* only."

"We hear much of the value of effort. That theory must be entirely repudiated, for he who says *effort* says *will*, and if the will is brought into play, imagination may run counter to it and bring about exactly contrary results."

"Always *think* that what you have to do *is easy*, if it is at all possible of being done. Then you will not expend any more strength than just what is necessary. If you think it is difficult, you will spend many times more strength than is actually required to perform it—you simply waste strength."

"Christian martyrs died with smiles upon their lips. They did not suffer the full extent of those awful tortures; but, holding clearly in mind the *image of the crown of life* which awaited them, they really experienced the heavenly joy which was soon to be theirs, not thinking of anything else."

"A person wants to do such and such a thing, but, *imagining that he is not able to accomplish it*, he does exactly the contrary to that which he wants to do. Dizziness is a striking example of this. Suppose a person is walking on a very narrow path, bordering a steep precipice. At first he thinks nothing of it; but suddenly, the *idea* comes to him that he *may tumble* over the edge. If he has the misfortune to look down, he is lost. The *image of a fall* has taken root in his mind; he feels himself attracted toward the abyss by an invisible force which becomes more and more insistent, the greater his efforts at resistance; finally he gives way and down he goes. This is the cause of most accidents in the Alps."

"*Physically you respond to the mental picture produced by your imagination; unwholesome thoughts are like an abyss that attracts those unable to resist.*"

"Repeat twenty times, morning and evening: *Every day, in every way, I am getting better and better.* It is the same remedy for everybody in the world. It is so simple and so easy. Almost too easy, isn't it? However, this is important: if you have the thought in your mind that you *are sick*, you surely will be. If you think you *are going to be cured*, it is sure to happen. It is the *certainty* that you are about to recover, that brings results, *not* the *hope*."

"*Patience* and *perseverance* are necessary in *autosuggestion*, as well as in everything else."

27-2-1917. Yes, yesterday I passed the 60th milestone and am on my way to be a septuagenarian; but unless a bomb or a 45 Colt bars my way, I do not in tend to stop there, and I'll carry my years lightly. *That is my idea and it will manifest itself.*

EMILE COUÉ.

Selected Comments

"Formerly it was believed that hypnotism could only be applied, successfully, to nervous diseases. Its power and influence go much further than that. It is true that hypnotism acts through the nervous system as intermediary; but the nervous system controls the whole organism. The muscles are made to move by the nerves; the nerves regulate the circulation of the blood by their direct action on the heart and by their action on the blood vessels which they dilate or contract. Therefore, the nerves act on all the organs and, by their intermediary action, may influence diseased organs."

Doctor Paul Joire,
President of the Society of Universal Psychological Studies.
(Bull. 4 of the S. L. P. A.)

"As an aid to recovery, mental influence is a powerful adjunct. It is a factor of the first order which we cannot afford to neglect, since in medicine as well as in every other branch of human activity, it is the *spiritual forces* that lead the world."

Dr. Louis Renon,
Lecturing Professor of the Faculty of Medicine of Paris and Physician at the Necker Hospital. (Bull. 3 of the S. L. P. A.)

"Never lose sight of this great principle in *autosuggestion*: OPTIMISM ALWAYS, AND IN SPITE OP EVERYTHING! EVEN IF EVENTS DO NOT SEEM TO JUSTIFY IT."

Rene Brabois, (Bull. II of the S. L. P. A.)

"Suggestion, sustained by faith, is a formidable force."

Dr. A. L., Paris, July, 1920.

"To have and to inspire unshakeable confidence, one must act with the assurance which only *perfect sincerity* can give; to possess such assurance and sincerity you must place the good of others above your own interests."

"*Culture of Moral Force*" by C. Baudouin.

M. Emile Coué
at Work in His Clinic

————

The old town of *Nancy* thrills at the mention of the name of *Coué*. People of every rank and class flock to him and all are received with an equally benevolent regard, which at once starts many along the way towards recovery. But the deeply touching part is to see, at the close of the session, people who came in bent and gloomy, with an almost hostile feeling (caused by pain), go away glad, happy, unconstrained and often radiant with joy—no longer in pain.

Smiling and goodnatured, with a cheerfulness that is his secret, *Mr. Coué* holds, so to speak, the hearts of his patients in the hollow of his hand. One by one he addresses the crowd of people who attend his clinic, talking to them as follows:

"Well, Madam, what is your complaint? Oh! you look too much for the why and wherefore. What does it matter to you what causes your pain. You suffer—that is enough. I will show you how you can get rid of your pain."

"And you, my dear sir, your varicose sore is improving already. That's fine, that's fine. Do you know, you have been here only twice? I congratulate you on having gotten such good results in so short a time. If you continue to make your *autosuggestion* properly, you will soon be entirely cured. You say that you have had this ulcer for ten years. What's the difference? You might have had that sore for twenty years or more, but it will heal up just the same."

"And you. You say that you have not improved at all. Do you know why? Simply because you have no *confidence in yourself.* When I say that you are better, you begin to feel better at once, don't you Why? Because you believe in me. Believe now in yourself and you will get just as good results."

"Oh! Madam. Not so many details, I beg you. In looking for details you create them and you would need a list a yard long to hold all your maladies. As a matter of fact it is your *mental outlook* which is wrong. Now, just make up your mind that you are going to get better and you will be better very soon. I am going to show you how to make your *autosuggestions*. It's as simple and as plain as the Gospel."

"You say you have an attack of nerves, every week. All right. You do as I tell you to and from now on you will not have them any more."

"You have been a sufferer from constipation for a long while. What does the time matter? You say, for forty years. Yes, I heard you, but nevertheless it is true that you can be cured *to-morrow*; do you hear, *tomorrow*! On condition, of course, that you do just what I tell you to do, and that you do it just as I show you."

"Ah! You suffer from glaucoma, Madam. I cannot absolutely promise a complete cure of that; I am not quite sure. But that does not mean that a cure is impossible, for I have seen a lady, of Chalons-sur-Saone, and another one, of Toul, cured."

"Well, Mademoiselle, as you have not had any nervous attacks since the last time you came here, and before that you used to have them every day, you are cured. Nevertheless, come and see me once in a while so that I may keep you moving along in the right direction."

"Your feeling of oppression will vanish just as soon as your lesions have disappeared and when you assimilate your food properly. That will all come about, in good time, but don't put the cart before the horse. It is the same with oppression as with heart trouble, both generally disappear pretty quickly."

Speaking to a child (in a clear and commanding voice): "Shut your eyes. I do not talk to you about lesions or anything of the kind; you would not understand it, anyway.

The pain in your chest is going and you don't feel like coughing any more."

To one who complains of *fatigue*: "Well, I have the same complaint. There are days when I, too, am tired of receiving people; nevertheless I receive them all day long. Don't say: *'I can't help it.'* One can always rise above one's self."

(Explanation. The *idea of being tired* brings about that languid feeling of fatigue; but, the *idea of having a duty to perform* always gives us the necessary strength to do it. The spirit *can* and *must* remain master of the animal nature.)

"Whatever may be the cause that prevents your walking, it is going to disappear, bit by bit, every day. You know the old proverb: *Heaven helps those who help themselves*. Stand up for a little while, several times each day, supporting yourself between two people. Do not say to yourself: *'My kidneys are too weak, I can't do it,'* but say aloud and with a firm voice: *I am, I can, I can*."

"After you have repeated *'Every day, in every way, I am getting better and better,'* you add: 'The persons that have been following me, do not follow me now; they *cannot* follow me any more'."

"What I have been telling you is very true: It is enough for you *to think* that you have no more pain, for the pain to disappear. Therefore, please do not think that it might come again; otherwise it surely will come back." (A woman murmurs: 'What *patience* he has, what a wonderfully painstaking man!')

"Whatever we think comes true for us. We must, therefore, *not think anything detrimental to ourselves.* Think: *My trouble is disappearing,* in the same way as you thought that you could not separate your hands when I told you that you could not. The more often you say to yourself: *'I will not'* the more often the very contrary thing comes to pass. You must think and say: *'It is going away.'* Close your hand and think very firmly: *'I cannot open it any more'* and you will be unable to do so. Try it and you will see how little your *will* has to do with the matter."

(Explanation. This is the pivoting point of the entire method. In order to make suggestions to yourself, the will must be completely eliminated. Work on your imagination only, for if there be conflict between the will and the imagination, the will is beaten every time.)

"Ah! to *'will'* and to *'desire'* is not the same thing."

"To become stronger as you become older may seem to be paradoxical, but it is true."

(A case of diabetes): "Continue to use also therapeutic treatments. I am quite willing to make *suggestions* to you, but I do not promise to cure you." (Note: I have seen diabetes cured several times and, what is still more extraordinary, the albumen diminished and even disappeared completely from the urine of certain patients.)

"This obsession of yours appears to be something of a real nightmare; the people you detested are becoming friends; you are going to like them and they will like you."

Then, requesting his patients to close their eyes, he gave them the little suggestive discourse which you will find in the text for "Practitioners." That little discourse finished, he addresses himself again to each patient separately, saying a few pleasant words regarding their individual illnesses:

"You, my dear sir, are in pain, but I tell you that from this day on, that, which causes the pain, is going to disappear. No matter whether it is called *arthritis* or whether it goes by any other name, your *Unconscious self* will do the thing needful to banish the cause; and as the cause is being removed, little by little, the pain also will vanish and in a short time there will be nothing left of it but the memory."

"Your stomach does not function properly, it is more or less distended. Well! As I told you just now, your digestive organs are going to work better and better, the distention of your stomach is also going to disappear, by and by. As your entire system regains force and elasticity, your stomach will benefit thereby and slowly get back into proper form to carry out, more and more easily, the movements necessary to pass the nourishment it contains, into the intestines. At the same time the pouch formed by the enlarged stomach will diminish in size; the food will no longer stagnate in that pouch and, consequently, fermentation will disappear."

"To you, Mademoiselle, I say that whatever lesions you may have in your liver, your organism is doing whatever is necessary to cause those lesions to heal up, more and more every day. By degrees, the symptoms from which you now suffer will lessen, and finally disappear entirely. Your liver is going to function, more and more in a normal way, secreting an alkaline bile which is no longer acidulous, but right in quantity and quality, so that it will pass into the intestinal tract in proper condition, and aid intestinal digestion."

"My child, you just listen: Every time you feel another attack coming on, you will hear my voice saying to you, with lightning-like rapidity: *No, No,* my friend, you are not going to have that attack! It will be gone before it really comes."

"I have told you and I repeat, my dear sir, that your varicose sore is going to heal. From this day on interlacing granulations will form at the bottom of your ulcer and growing, they will gradually fill the hole now existing. At the same time the ledges will reapproach each other in every direction both in height and width until they touch and heal up altogether."

"You have a rupture, you say. Well! It can and it will be cured. Your *Unconscious self* will act in such a way that the rupture which exists in your peritoneum is going to heal up by degrees. The hole will get smaller and smaller every day until it is completely closed and you have no rupture any more."

"And you, my dear sir, who have glaucoma (or a cataract, or some sort of an affection of the eyes), I tell you that from this day on, the lesions which you have in your eyes will begin to heal up and as they do so by degrees, you will notice that your eyes are getting better and better and you will be able to see farther and much more clearly."

"You say you have eczema (or an affection of the skin). This affection will disappear rapidly; I said *rapidly*, you understand? The cause which brought about this affection is going to vanish and, naturally, the cause being removed, the symptoms will vanish likewise. If there is smarting or itching in the affected parts you will notice that it lessens day by day. If there is a slight discharge, it will also be less and less every day; in short, as your skin peels off in the form of scales, you will find it replaced by a new elastic skin of natural color."

Enteritis. "The intestinal inflammation will diminish gradually and the *glaires* and membranes which sometimes accompany your stools, will at the same time become less frequent until they stop altogether and you will be cured."

Anemia. "Your blood is becoming more and more rich, red and abundant until it has improved to the natural state of a healthy person. In this way your anemia and all the annoying conditions that follow in its train will have entirely vanished."

"Every time you begin to have pains say right away: *It passes, it passes.* Say it quickly, rapidly, like a barrage-fire. You must learn how to use *autosuggestion* and after having had a few lessons, you will not need me anymore, unless you *think* that you need me."

"The experiments have been very successful. If you do not get any sleep, it is because you are making efforts. It is enough to say: *I am going to sleep, I am going to sleep,* humming it like the sound of a flying bee. If this proves unsuccessful it is simply because you are not doing it right."

"All that is periodical is self-acquired. When the time arrives which is called 'change of life,' all ladies have one complaint or another. From childhood they have heard it said: Aunt Gertrude has it, Cousin Mary has it, etc., and they assume naturally that they too are going to have it."

"To say: Provided I do not have neuralgia, is as much as saying that you expect to have it. Do not give a thought to an ailment of any kind, otherwise that which you 'expect' and are afraid of, is going to happen."

"You are constipated because you *think* you are. Just *think* the *contrary* and the contrary will happen."

"These fears and aversions must disappear. You have in yourself the instrument of your recovery. Drive them away, let them drop like the crumbs from your table. Nobody in the world can exercise any influence on you, unless you *permit it*. Don't come next time to tell me that you are not better, you *will be better.* And do not use your *will*, sapristi, do not even use the words: *'I will.'* I forbid you (if there is anything at all to forbid)."

"If you have a broken bone go to the hospital this morning. Suggestion does not re-set or repair broken bones, but directs and controls the organs, muscles, nerves, etc."

"Do you follow your diet for albumen?" Patient: "I do not like the milk-food." Mr. Coué: *"Well, imagine that you do like it."*

"As regards those itchings (you have been here three times) impress the thought on your mind that they will never come back again. If you *are afraid* that they are going to occur again, they surely will. Even after you have improved, continue to see me from time to time in order that I may encourage you to keep yourself in the right direction."

Patient: "One may force one's self to think, doctor?"

Mr. Coué: "No need to force yourself to practice the 'method'; that comes quite naturally. It is the same with me, you know."

Patient: "I cannot say: *'I cannot'* when I think *'I can'*."

Mr. Coué: "Do as I tell you. It's I who give *you* a lesson, not you to me."

Bronchitis: "You have bronchitis and are taking the Valda tablets. That's all right to calm irritation. Suggestion will make the *cause* of irritation disappear."

"You have seen your doctor about it; follow the diet he has prescribed for you. Madam, you must follow the treatment prescribed by your doctor and *make suggestions at the same time*. The one does not prevent or prohibit the other; on the contrary, I too prescribe for you."

"There is no *healer* here, but a gentleman who *teaches* you what to do to heal yourself."

Neuralgia: "Whatever the cause may be for your head-aches, your organism will do all that is necessary to make that cause disappear by degrees and, of course, in the same measure as the cause does disappear, your neuralgia will be less frequent and less violent until, in the near future, it will have vanished altogether. You feel, by the way, every time I pass my hand across your forehead, it takes away some of the pain; and in a moment, when you open your eyes, you will find that you are entirely free from it."

Patient: "I suffocate, especially in hot weather."
Mr. Coué: "You have seen your doctor?"
Patient: "I have seen six doctors. They said it is nervousness, but they did nothing for it."
Mr. Coué: "Yes, it is nervousness, but we are going to help you to get rid of it."

After everybody has thus been passed in review Mr. Coué tells his patients to open their eyes, and says: "You have heard the advice I have just given you. Well! In order to transform my suggestions into realities, here is what you must do: As long as you live, every morning before rising, and every evening as soon as you are in bed, close your eyes and repeat, twenty times, with your lips (this is indispensable) and counting mechanically on a string with twenty knots in it, the following phrase: *Every day, in every way, I am getting better and better.*

"Do not think of anything in particular as the words: '*in every way*' apply to everything. Make this *autosuggestion* with confidence, with faith, with the *certainty* that you are going to obtain what you desire. The greater the faith of the patient, the greater and the more rapid will be the results.

"Moreover, if at any time during the day or night you feel any physical or mental discomfort, say to yourself that you will not consciously contribute toward it, but that you are going to compel it to disappear. Then isolate yourself as much as possible and pass your hand across your forehead, if it is something mental, or over the painful part, if it is something physical, and repeat with extreme rapidity, moving the lips: '*It passes, it passes, it passes*' as long as is necessary. With a little practice the mental or physical discomfort will disappear in twenty to twenty-five seconds. Repeat again whenever necessary."

"In this as well as in other *autosuggestions* it is necessary to act with equal confidence, equal faith, and above all *without effort*."

Mr. Coué says further: "If formerly you have been in the habit of making, unconsciously to yourself, bad autosuggestions, now knowing what I have taught you, you must not let those bad, unconscious autosuggestions occur again. And if in spite of all I have said and done, you still persist in making them, then you have only yourselves to blame and had better strike your breast arid say: 'Mea culpa, mea culpa, mea maxima culpa'."

Now, if a grateful admirer of the work and of the founder of the "method" may be permitted to say a few words:

Since Mr. Coué tells us that it is the *imagination* which makes us act and that this is the basis of his "method," I would like to add: The pillars of his structure are the *thousands of cures obtained*; and the crowning part, the most magnificently crowning part, is his noble admission, *the power is in you, in each of you*, constituting not only an immense benefit for suffering humanity, but also a tribute to its creator.

Henceforth, each can adapt this "method" to his own personal creed. If we are religious, it will help us to remove obstacles which we unconsciously believe to exist between God and ourselves. And for believers as well as skeptics, free-thinkers and heathen, the *Coué method* teaches us how to deliver ourselves from mental or physical pain that is unjustified, by use of the simple yet marvelous process of Coué: *It passes!*

As for those who reject the "method," ignorant of the secret of its force, I will ask one question: "Do you also reject electric light because you (as well as the greatest and most learned professors) do not know the secret of the power of electricity?"

Oh! Now, you *don't know*, you *cannot know* what this blessed method can do and will do to restore you mentally and physically. *But in living and practising it, you will know it.* It is sure to help you to gain the victory, the mastery of yourself.

E. Vs . . . OER.

Letters

Extracts from Letters to M. Coué

AUGUST, 1916.

The final results of the English secondary Certificate have been posted only these two hours but I hasten to inform you of the fact, at least so far as it concerns me. I passed the oral exams with flying colors and scarcely felt a trace of nervousness, which formerly caused me such intolerable sensations of nausea before examinations began. During these latter tests I was astonished at my own calm, which gave those who listened to me the impression of perfect self-possession on my part. In short, the very tests which I most feared, contributed most to my success. The Jury placed me *second*, and I am infinitely grateful for your help which undoubtedly gave me an advantage over the other candidate, etc.

Mile. V ., Professor at the Lyceum*.

---

* This concerns a young lady who, because of extraordinary nervousness, had failed in her examinations in 1915. The great nervousness having disappeared under the influence of *autosuggestion*, she passed successfully, winning the *second place*, among more than two hundred competitors.

NANCY, AUGUST, 1917.

It is with the greatest pleasure that I write this to thank you from my heart for the great benefit I have derived from your method. Before I went to you I had great difficulty in walking, even so short a distance as one hundred yards, without becoming breathless, while now I can go miles without fatigue. Several times a day, very easily, and in 40 minutes, I walk from the rue de Bord-de-l'Eau to rue de Glacis—about four kilometres. The asthma, from which I suffered so much, has *disappeared* almost completely. Please accept most sincere thanks from yours gratefully,

Paul Chenot, *Rue de Strasbourg* 141.

HAUTE-SAONE, MAY, 1918.

I don't know how to thank you. Thanks to you I can say that I am almost entirely cured, but merely waited for complete cure before expressing my gratitude to you, but will wait no longer. I was afflicted with two varicose ulcers, one on each foot. The one on my right foot, which was as big as my hand, is entirely healed. It seemed to disappear as if by magic. For weeks I had been confined to my bed. Shortly after the receipt of your letter* the

---

* NB. It is noteworthy that this lady has never seen Mr. Coué; it was due to a letter, which the latter wrote her on the 15th of April, that she obtained the results mentioned above in her letter of May 3rd.

ulcer healed, so that I was able to get up. The one on the left foot is not entirely healed yet but will be soon. Every night and every morning I repeat the phrase, as directed, with complete confidence. I must also tell you that my legs were as hard as stone and I could not bear the slightest touch on them. Now I can press them without the least pain and I can walk again. What joy!

Madame Ligny, *Maileroncourt-Charette.*

PONT-A-MOUSSON, FEBRUARY, 1920.
I write to express my wholehearted gratitude to you, for, thanks to you, I have escaped the risks of a dangerous operation. More: you have saved my life. Your method of *autosuggestion*, alone, has done what medicines and treatments could not do for that terrible intestinal obstruction, from which I had suffered for 19 days. From the moment I began to follow your instructions and applied your excellent principles, my system functioned quite naturally.

Madame S.

SAINT-DIE, FEBRUARY, 1920.
I do not know how to thank you enough for the joy and happiness I have in being cured. For more than fifteen years I suffered from asthma. Every night I almost suffocated. Thanks to your splendid method, and especially since I had the privilege of being present at one of your

sittings, these attacks have disappeared as if by magic. It is truly a *miracle*, for all the doctors who attended me, assured me that there was no cure for asthma.

Mme. V.

Sens, June, 1920.

I have been waiting to write you until I had seen the uncle of my husband, Professor M., physician-in-chief of the Tenon Hospital. He was greatly astonished to see his nephew in such excellent health after the latter had been suffering from suffocating asthmatic attacks every night for fifteen years. We had tried everything. All the great medical lights had treated him, but the entire medical science was unable to help him. You alone, dear sir, have succeeded where everybody and everything else failed. Yes, my husband is now well. He is not yet completely cured, but one must not forget that his disease is of fifteen years' standing.

Dr. J., who was amazed at the results obtained by your method, has undoubtedly written to you, and Dr. M. desires very much to make your personal acquaintance; he has been a professor and member of the Faculty for twenty years. He is happy, very happy, that his nephew is almost entirely cured. Whenever you go again to Paris he will be greatly pleased to see you. Dr. B., also, calls from time to time on his ex-patient; it was after trying everything possible that I went to you.

Mme. M.

VINCENNES, MAY, 1920.

I am writing to you with all my heart to thank you for having brought to my knowledge a new therapeutic method; a wonderful instrument which seems to act like the magic wand of a fairy, since, thanks to the simplest means, it brings about the most extraordinary results.

From the first I had a lively interest in your experiments and, after my own personal successes with your method, I eagerly apply it at every opportunity and have since become a fervent and enthusiastic adept.

Dr. Vachet.

TOUL, MAY, 1920.

During eight years I have suffered from displacement of the womb. Having used your method of *autosuggestion* for five months, I am now completely cured and really do not know how to thank you sufficiently.

Mme. Soulier, *Place du Marche.*

PARIS, APRIL, 1920.

I have suffered horribly for eleven years without interruption. Every night I had attacks of asthma. I suffered also from insomnia and general weakness which made occupation of any kind impossible. Mentally I was depressed, restless and worried, seeing mountains where there were but mole-hills. I had taken any amount of treatments without success and even had undergone, in Switzerland, the removal of the spongy bones of the nose, likewise without effect. In November 1918, I became worse in consequence of a great sorrow. While my husband was at Corfu (as an officer on board a battleship) I lost our only son, in six days, from influenza. He was a lovely child of ten years, and the sunshine of our life. Alone and overwhelmed with sorrow, I reproached myself bitterly for not having been able to protect and save our treasure. I was nearly insane and wanted to die. When my husband returned (in February), he took me to another doctor, who prescribed various remedies along with the waters of Mont-Dore. I spent the month of August at that place but on my return the attacks of asthma recurred, as before. I realized, with despair, that I was going from bad to worse *in every respect*. At that critical time I had the pleasure of meeting you. Although I hardly expected any good from it, I attended your conferences during the month of October and I am very happy to say that by the end of November I was cured. Insomnia, depression, gloomy thoughts have disappeared as if by magic, I am now well, strong, and full of courage. With my physical health restored, I have also recovered my mental equilibrium and, if it were not for the ineffaceable effect of the loss of my child which keeps my mother-heart still bleeding, I would say that I am entirely well and, so far as possible, happy. I wish to goodness I had met you before. My child would then have known a cheerful and courageous mother.

A thousand thanks, Mr. Coué. Thank you again and again.

Most gratefully yours,
E. I., *Rue de Lille*.

JANUARY, 1920.

I can now take up again the struggle which I maintained for thirty years, until exhausted. I found in you, last August, wonderful and providential help. Returning to our dear Lorraine, I arrived ill and with a heart full of sorrow. I dreaded the shock which I would feel at the sight of all the ruins and distress. I went away comforted and in good health. I was almost insane—unfortunately I am not religious. I longed for someone to help and comfort me. By a lucky chance I met you at my sister's and you gave me the very help and consolation I sought. I now work with new spirit and suggest to my *unconscious self* to reestablish my physical equilibrium. I have no doubt that I shall regain my former good health. I have already noticed some improvement. You will better understand my gratitude when I tell you that, suffering from diabetes and a renal complication, I have had several attacks of glaucoma; but my eyes are now recovering slowly. My eyesight has in the meantime become almost normal and my general health is much better.

Mlle. Th., *Professor at the Young Ladies' College of Ch... s.*

I read my thesis with success and have been awarded the highest mark, together with the congratulations of the Jury. Of all these honors a large share is due to you, and I do not forget it. My only regret is that you were not present to hear your name referred to with warm and sympathetic interest by so distinguished a Jury. You may rest assured that the doors of the University have been thrown wide open to your teaching. Do not thank me, please, for I owe you far more than you owe me.

Charles Baudouin,
Professor at the Institut J. J. Rousseau, Geneva.

PARIS, MARCH, 1920.
I admire your undaunted courage and am sure that it will help to give to many minds an intelligent and useful direction. I must confess that I personally have benefitted by your teaching, and am applying it to my patients, also. At the Clinic we try to apply your method collectively, and have already obtained visible results.

Dr. Bertillon.

BRUXELLES, MARCH, 1920.
I have received your kind letter and also your very interesting lecture. I am glad to see that you make a rational

fusion between *hetero* and *autosuggestion*; I note particularly the passage in which you say that the Will must not intervene in *autosuggestion*. That is what a number of teachers and users of autosuggestion, including a great many physicians do not understand. I consider that, likewise, an absolute distinction should be made between *autosuggestion* and *the training of the will.*

Dr. van Velsen.

Cesson-Saint-Brieuc.

I wonder what you must think of me? Forgotten you? Never! Best assured that I shall always think of you with deep and grateful affection. I must tell you that your teachings are more and more effective with me; I do not pass a day without using *autosuggestion* with increased success, and bless you every day; your method is the true one. Thanks to it I control myself better every day—I assimilate your directions and feel myself stronger. I am sure that you would have difficulty in recognizing in me, so active in spite of 66 years, the poor creature who was so often ailing and who is only now beginning to feel well, thanks to you and to your guidance. May the Lord bless you, my dear sir, for it is the sweetest thing to do good to others. You are doing much good; I do a little and I thank God for it.

Mme. M.

RICHEMONT, JUNE, 1920.

Am feeling better and better since following your method of *autosuggestion*. I ask you to please accept my most sincere thanks. The lesion of the lungs has disappeared, the heart is better and there is no more albumen; in short I am feeling fine.

Mme. Lemaitre.

MADRID.

Your booklet and your lecture have interested us very much. For the good of humanity it would be desirable to have them printed in several languages, so that they might reach every race and country and thus make happy a greater number of unfortunate people, who suffer because they are using wrongly this mighty and almost divine faculty which we call *imagination* and which is most important to man, as you affirm and prove so clearly and judiciously. I had already read many books on the Will and I have also quite an arsenal of formulas, thoughts, aphorisms, etc. Your teaching is conclusive. I do not think that anyone ever before condensed so intelligently these formulas into "compressed tablets of self-confidence," as I call your healing phrases.

Don Enrique C .

From Letters to Mme. Emile Leon,
(*Disciple of M. Coué*)

PARIS.

For some time I have been wanting to write and thank you most sincerely for having brought to my knowledge this method of *autosuggestion*. Thanks to your good advice the attacks of nerves, to which I was subject, have entirely disappeared, and I am certain that I am completely cured. Moreover, I feel myself surrounded by a superior force which is an unfaltering guide which aids me to overcome, with ease, the difficulties of life.

Mme. F., 4, rue de Bougainville.

PARIS.

Amazed at the results obtained by practising *autosuggestion* as you taught me, I wish to thank you with all my heart. It is now a year since I was completely cured of articular rheumatism of the right shoulder, which bothered me for eight years, and also of chronic bronchitis from which I had suffered still longer. Numerous doctors declared that I was incurable, but thanks to your treatment, I am again in perfect health and have the assurance of power to conserve it.

Mme. L. T. 4, rue du Laos.

PARIS, JUNE 17, 1920.

I must tell you of the excellent results which Mr. Coué's method has produced in my case, and thank you for your valuable help. I have always been uremic and consequently in poor health, but after the death of my husband I grew still worse. My kidneys did not act, I could not stand upright and suffered from nervousness and aversions. All have disappeared and I am a different person. There are no more pains, I have more endurance and am more cheerful. My friends hardly know me. I intend to spread the news of this wonderful method which is so clear, so simple, so beneficial, and expect the very best results for myself from its continued use.

M. L. D.

PARIS, OCTOBER 3, 1920.

I cannot find words to thank you sufficiently for teaching me your splendid method. What happiness you have brought to me. I thank God who guided me to make your acquaintance; you have completely transformed my life. Formerly I suffered terribly at each monthly period and was obliged to stay in bed; now it is quite regular and painless. It is the same with my digestion; I am no longer obliged to live on milk, as I used to and there are no more pains, at which I am very happy. My husband is astonished to find that, when traveling, I am free from headaches, while formerly I had to take tablets all the time. Now, thanks to you, dear madame, I have no need of medicine any more. But I do not forget to repeat twenty times every morning and evening the phrase which you have taught me: 'Every day, in every way, I am getting better and better.'

B. P.

Paris.

I am delightfully surprised at the results which I have obtained, and am still obtaining daily, by use of the excellent method which you taught me of *conscious auto-suggestion*. I was mentally and physically sick. Now I am well and almost always in high spirits. My depression has given way to constant cheerfulness and I certainly do not complain of the change. Sapristi! How wretched I used to be. I was unable to digest anything, whatever it was; now I digest everything and the intestinal functions are natural. Moreover, I suffered from insomnia and now the nights are not long enough. I could not work at all; now I am capable of doing all kinds of hard work. Of all my ailments nothing remains but an occasional slight touch of rheumatism, but I am sure that by the continued use of your splendid method that also will disappear as everything else did. I cannot find proper words to express my deep gratitude to you.

Mme. Friry, *Boulevard Malesherbes.*

From Letters to Mlle. Kaufmant,
(*Disciple of M. Coué*)

NICE, 1918.

Feeling better and better since I have followed the method of *autosuggestion* which you taught me, I consider it my duty to thank you most heartily. I am now qualified to speak of the great and undeniable advantages of this method, as it alone put me on the road to recovery. My illness consisted of a lesion in the lungs, which caused spitting of blood and in addition I had no appetite for anything, vomited daily, became a mere skeleton and suffered from obstinate constipation. The spitting of blood lessened almost immediately and soon stopped entirely; the vomiting ceased, constipation disappeared, my appetite came back and in two months I gained twelve pounds.

In the presence of such results, observed not only by my parents and friends but also by the doctor who attended me for several months, it is impossible to deny the good effects of *autosuggestion* and I must declare publicly that I owe my return to life to your method.

You are authorized to use my name if I can be of service to others. With deep gratitude I beg to remain, yours most gratefully

Jeanne Gilli, 15 *Avenue Borriglione.*

NICE, MARCH, 1919.

I consider it a sacred duty to express to you my deep gratitude for having taught me your method of *autosuggestion* from which I derived such great benefits. Thanks to you, dear madame, I suffer no longer from those frequent and agonizing palpitations of the heart which made me feel at times that it was about to stop beating. I have also regained my appetite which I had lost for months. As a hospital nurse I have to thank you for the almost miraculous recovery of one of my patients who was seriously afflicted with tuberculosis and vomited much blood. His family and myself feared that the worst might happen at any moment when merciful heaven sent you to him. After your very first visit the spitting of blood ceased, his appetite returned and, after you had made a few more visits to his sickbed, all the organs gradually resumed their normal functions. Finally we had the pleasant surprise of seeing him arrive one day at your private clinic where, before those present, he himself told the story of his wonderful cure, ascribing it to your personal intervention.

I thank you from the very bottom of my heart.

Gratefully yours,
A. Kettner, 26, Avenue Borriglione.

LIVERDUN, AUGUST 30, 1920.

From day to day I have put off writing to thank you for the cure of my little Sylvain. I was in despair when the doctors told me that there was nothing more to be done, except to give him a chance by sending him to the sanatorium at Arcachon or Juicoot, near Dunkirk. I was about to send him there when Mme. Collard advised going to see you first. Feeling skeptical about it, I hesitated but now I have the proof of your science; my Sylvain has completely recovered. He now eats with good appetite, his pimples and glands are completely cured and, most extraordinary of all, since our first visit to you, he has not coughed any more, not even once. Since last June he has gained six pounds. I can never thank you enough and will proclaim publicly the benefits received from your treatment.

Mme. Poirson.

NANCY, NOVEMBER 4, 1920.

How can I prove to you my heartfelt gratitude? You, Mademoiselle, have saved my life. I had heart disease which caused me terrible suffering from incessant attacks of suffocation; they were so violent that I had no rest, day or night, notwithstanding daily injections of morphine. All food caused instant vomiting. I suffered also from violent pains in my head, which became so swollen that I lost my sight. I was in terrible plight, my whole organism being in a most lamentable state; there was an abscess on the liver; my doctor tried everything in his power: letting blood, scarified cupping, needle-pricks, poultices, ice, and every possible medicine, without result. Finally he advised me to consult you.

After your first visits the heart attacks diminished in violence and became less frequent; soon they ceased entirely. I was able to rest and, to my great relief, could soon sleep throughout the night, without waking. The pains in the liver ceased. I began to enjoy my food again and digested it perfectly, experiencing once more a feeling of hunger which I had not known for months. The pains in the head stopped and my eyes are quite cured, so that I am now able to busy myself a little, manually. Each time you paid me a visit I felt better, my organs gradually resuming their normal functions. I was not the only one to observe the wonderful improvement; the doctor who came to see me every week found me very much better and, finally recovery came. I was able to get up after having been confined to bed for eleven months. I rose without the least discomfort, even without dizziness, and at the end of another fortnight I went out for a walk. I am indebted to you alone for my recovery and the doctor candidly admits that, for all the good his medicines had done me, I might just as well have taken none at all. After having been given up by two doctors, it is a pleasure indeed to be alive and well again. My recovery is so complete that I can now eat meat and also take a pound of bread daily. How can I thank you? I repeat, it is to your good suggestions that I owe my life.

Jeanne Grosjean.

NANCY, NOVEMBER 16, 1920.

Personally the *science of autosuggestion*—which, indeed, I consider entirely as a science—has been of great benefit to me; my interest in it continues, particularly, because I find it to be the means of exercising true charity.

In 1915, when for the first time I was present at one of Mr. Coué's lectures, I confess I was entirely skeptical; but in the face of facts, repeated *a hundred times* in my very presence, I had to bow before the evidence and recognize that *autosuggestion* does act, although of course in different degrees, oh organic diseases. Strangely, the only cases in which I have known it to fail (and those were very rare) were of a nervous nature such as neurasthenia and imaginary maladies.

It is needless to tell you again that Mr. Coué insists, like yourself, but even more strongly, on this point: 'that he does not perform any miracles, that he does not cure anybody, but that he only teaches people to cure themselves.' I confess that, on this point, I am still a little incredulous; for if Mr. Coué does not actually cure personally, he is most decidedly a powerful aid to recovery. He puts heart and new courage into the sick and afflicted and teaches them never to despair. He has an uplifting influence and guides them to moral heights hitherto beyond them and which, in their everyday materialism, they never even conceived of.

The deeper I go into the study of *autosuggestion*, the the better I am able to understand the divine law of confidence and love which Christ taught us: *Love thy neighbor as thyself*; give him a little of your heart and of your moral force; help him rise if he has fallen; heal him if he is sick. That is the 'Gift of God' of which Jesus speaks to the good Samaritan. *Autosuggestion* is a beneficial and comforting science and its application, from my Christian point of view, tends to make us better understand that we are all the children of God, that we all have within us unsuspected, undreamed of forces which, rightly directed, serve to elevate us morally and to heal us physically. Those who do not know your *science* or have merely a slight inkling of it, should not pass judgment unless and until they have witnessed the magnificent results obtained by *autosuggestion*, and the great good it does.

M. L. D.

All for Everyone

By MME. EMILE LÉON, *disciple of Mr. Coué.*

f you have been privileged to enjoy an inestimably great benefit, and one that is within the reach of all, although most are ignorant of it, is it not an absolute and urgent duty, for you who do know, to spread that knowledge broadcast? Particularly when everyone who learns of it can appropriate to himself its amazing benefits, as is true of the Coué "method."

To relieve pain is wonderful, very wonderful; but how much more wonderful is it to guide those, who now suffer, into full enjoyment of a new life?

Last April, at Paris, we had the pleasure of a visit from Mr. Coué; here are some gleanings from his talks:

Question of a Theist: "From a religious point of view I consider it unworthy to believe that the Eternal would let our obedience to His will depend on a trick, or mechanical process—what Mr. Coué calls *conscious autosuggestion*."
Answer: "Whether we wish to believe it or not, it is true that our imagination always overrules our will when the

latter is in conflict with the former. But we can lead the imagination into the right path—as indicated by our reason—by *consciously* employing the mechanical process which now we so often employ *unconsciously* to lead us the wrong way."

A thoughtful listener said: "Yes, it is true; *conscious autosuggestion* has in it the power to free us from ob stacks, created by ourselves, which act like a veil placed between God and ourselves; as a rag, suspended over a window, prevents the sun from shining into a room.

Question: How can we induce sufferers, who are near and dear to us, to make *good autosuggestions* which would free them from paint

Answer: Do not urge or lecture them about it. Simply remind them that I recommend that they make *autosuggestions*, with the certainty that they will obtain the result they want.

Question: How can one explain satisfactorily, to one's self and to others, this phenomenon—that the mere repetition of the same words: *"I am going to sleep," "It passes,"* etc., has the power to produce the desired effect, and so powerfully that the result is a *certainty?*

Answer: The repetition of the same words forces us to *think* them, and when we think them they *become true for us* and transform themselves into reality.

Question: How is one to conserve self-mastery as an inward power?

Answer: To be master of yourself it is enough to *think* that you are master; and in order to think it, you must *repeat it often*, but without any effort.

Question: And how is one to keep one's liberty of outward activity?
Answer: Self-mastery applies just as much physically as it does mentally.

Questioner: We cannot escape trouble or sadness, can we, if we do not do as we should? It would not be just and *autosuggestion* cannot, and ought not to prevent just suffering.
Mr. Coué (very seriously and affirmatively): Certainly and assuredly it ought not to be so, but it *often is*, at any rate for a time.

Question: Why did that patient, now cured, have those incessant and terrible attacks?
Answer: He expected those attacks; he feared them; hence he *provoked* them. If this gentleman will make up his mind *firmly* that he is not going to have any more attacks, he will not have them. But if he continues to think that he will have them, he certainly will have them.

Question: In what does your "method" differ from others?
Answer: The difference in my "method" is: that it is based on the principle that it is not the *will* which rules us, but the *imagination*. That is its fundamental basis.

Question: "Will you give me a summary of your "method" for Mme. R., who is writing an important work on the subject?

Answer: I can give you a summary of my method in a few words: Contrary to the common belief it is not our *will* which makes us act, but our *imagination* (which is an unconscious being). If it often happens that we do act as *we will*, it is because we *think*, at the same time, *that we can*. If that be not so, we do exactly the contrary of what we *willed* to do. For example: The more a person afflicted with insomnia *determines* to sleep, the more excited he gets; the more you try to remember a name which you seem to have forgotten, the more elusive it is. It only comes back to your mind if, instead of thinking *"I have forgotten,"* you replace that thought by *"I know it, I know it, I remember it."* The more we strive to suppress a burst of laughter, the more violently the laughter explodes. The more a person learning to ride a bicycle *wills* to avoid an obstacle, the straighter he runs right into it.

We must, therefore, endeavor to direct our imagination—which at present directs us. In this way we easily become, physically and mentally, masters of ourselves. How are we to arrive at this result? By the practice of *conscious autosuggestion*, which is based on this principle: Every idea, firmly implanted in our minds, tends to become true for us and to realize itself

Thus, if we desire something physical or mental, we can obtain it, sooner or later, provided we repeat rapidly and often, that the thing is going to happen, or is not going to happen, according as to whether it is something desirable or undesirable.

Everything is provided for in the general formula to be used morning and night: *Every day, in every way, I am getting better and better.*

Question: For those who are sad or who are in distress?
Answer: As long as you think *"I am sad,"* you cannot be gay; and in order to *think something* it is enough to say, without effort: *"I think this thing,"* etc. Pain or distress, no matter how violent it may be, will disappear. That I can affirm *positively.*

A man, bent with rheumatism, arrives, painfully dragging himself with the help of two canes. His face shows a dull expression of pain. As the room is filling up *Mr. Coué* enters and, after questioning this man, says to him: "Well. You say you have been suffering from rheumatism for thirty-two years and you cannot walk. Don't be afraid. It is not going to last that long again." Then, after the preliminary experiments: "Shut your eyes and repeat rapidly, very rapidly, moving your lips, the words *it is going . . . it is going*" (at the same time Mr. Coué passes his hand along the legs of the patient for about twenty seconds). "Now you do not suffer any more, get up and walk!" The sick man rises and walks. "Faster, faster, still faster! Now, since you are walking so well, run, my dear sir, run!" And the patient runs joyously, almost as if he had recovered his youth (to the great astonishment of himself and that of the many persons present at the clinic of Dr. Berillon, April 27th, 1920).

A lady declares: My husband suffered from suffocating attacks of asthma for many years; indeed, he had such difficulty in breathing that we feared a fatal issue. His doctor had given him up. He was almost entirely cured of his trouble after a single visit to Mr. Coué.

A young woman comes to thank Mr. Coué, with deep gratitude. Her physician, Dr. Vachet, who was with her in the consulting room, stated that she had suffered a long time from cerebral anemia. He had been unable to check this disease by the usual remedies, but it had disappeared entirely, as if by magic, with the use of *conscious autosuggestion*.

Another person, who as a result of having once suffered a fractured leg and could neither walk nor even limp along without pain, was able to walk normally at once. No more pain and no more limping. The hall thrills with interest and joyous shouts from grateful people, relieved or cured.

A doctor: "Autosuggestion is the great Power of Healing." He relies on the genius of Coué.

A former magistrate exclaimed enthusiastically: "I cannot put my appreciation into words! I think it is admirable!"

A society woman, overexcited by the disappearance of her sufferings, exclaims: "Oh! Mr. Coué, one would like to kneel to you . . . You are the good God . . ." Another lady, herself also very much impressed, set her fellow hearer right, by saying: "No, His ambassador."

An old lady: "It is delightful to be able, even when one is aged and fragile, to replace a feeling of general weakness and ill health by one of refreshment and general well-being. The method of Mr. Emile Coué can, I affirm, for I have experienced it myself, bring about that indescribably happy result which is all the more complete and lasting, as it relies on the all powerful force which is within us."

A truly sympathetic voice called him by the modest name he prefers to that of *"master"* i.e., *Professor* Coué.

A young woman, likewise very enthusiastic, says "Mr. Coué goes straight to his mark, attains it surely and delivers his patient. He raises generosity and knowledge to the highest pitch by leaving to the patient himself the *merit of his own deliverance*, teaching him at the same time the use of a most marvelous power."

A literary man, requested to write a little epitome of the beneficial "method", refused absolutely and stated emphatically that the simple phrase, *"it passes,"* is the epitome, since by its use, according to the "method," it causes all suffering to disappear. And the many thousands of sick folks who have been relieved or cured will not contradict him.

A lady who has suffered much declares: "In re-reading the 'method' more and more I find it superior to the more lengthy writings which it has inspired. Truly, there is nothing to be added and nothing to be taken away from the 'method.' It remains only to spread it. I shall do that in every way possible."

In conclusion I will say: Although Mr. Coué's modesty causes him to answer everyone:

"I have no magnetic fluid . . . I have no influence . . . I have never cured anybody . . . My disciples obtain the same results as myself . . ."

I can say in all sincerity: "Instructed as they are by this priceless 'method' they attempt to follow their master and instructor, and when, in some far distant future, the thrilling voice of the author is called to a higher sphere and can no longer teach them here below, the *'method,'* his work, will continue to contribute in helping, consoling and curing thousands and thousands of human beings. It will be *immortal*, and will be communicated by generous France to the entire world . . . for the man of letters was right. He knew how to express in one appropriate word this true, simple yet marvelous aid in conquering pain: *It passes!* There is the epitome."

Some Notes on the
Trip of Mr. Coué to Paris
(October, 1918)

———

The desire that the teachings of Mr. Coué in Paris, last October, should not be lost to others, has induced me to write them down. We will not mention at this time the great number of mental and physical sufferers who, under his treatment, have seen their troubles and pains lessen and disappear, but limit ourselves to a simple statement of a few of his teachings:

Question: How is it that I do not obtain better results in spite of using your method and formula?

Mr. Coué: Because there is, probably in the background of your mind an *unconscious doubt*, or because you make efforts. Remember please, that *efforts* are determined by the *will*. If you bring the will into play you run a serious risk of bringing the imagination into play at the same time, but in opposition to your wish, thus bringing about just the reverse of what you desire.

Question: What are we to do when something troubles us?

Answer: If something occurs to trouble you, repeat at once: "No, that does not trouble me at all, not at all; if anything it is rather agreeable to me." In short, the idea is to work yourself into a good frame of mind, rather than into a bad one.

Question: Are the preliminary experiments indispensable if they hurt the pride of the subject?

Answer: No, they are not indispensable, but they are *extremely useful*. Although they may seem childish to some people, they are, on the contrary, very serious. Indeed, they prove three things:

1. That every idea we have in our minds becomes *true* for us and has a tendency to transform itself into action.

2. That when a conflict occurs between the *imagination* and the *will*, it is always the imagination which gains the upper hand; and in that case we do precisely the contrary of what we want to do.

3. That it is easy to plant in our minds, *without any effort*, the idea which we wish to have there, since we have been able to think successively and without effort, first—"*I cannot*" and then—"*I can.*"

The preliminary experiments should not be repeated at home; alone, one is often unable to put one's self into the right physical and mental condition; you risk failure and in that case your self-confidence is shaken.

Question: When one is in pain one cannot help thinking of one's trouble.

Answer: Don't be afraid to think of it; on the contrary, think of it, but say to it: "I am not afraid of you." If you enter a home somewhere and a dog suddenly jumps at you barking, look straight into its eyes and it will not bite you. But if you are afraid and turn your back it will soon bury its teeth in your leg.

Question: But if one has to beat a retreat?

Answer: Then retreat step by step, going backwards, facing the dog.

Question: How can we *realize* what we desire?

Answer: By repeating often what you desire—for instance: "I am gaining poise," and you will; "My memory improves," and it certainly will improve; "I am able to control myself absolutely," and there is no question but that you will.

If you tell yourself the contrary, it is the contrary which is going to happen. What you tell yourself persistently *and very rapidly*, comes to pass (provided of course, that it is something natural.)

A Few Testimonials

One young lady to another: "How simple it all is! There is nothing to add to it; he seems to be inspired. Don't you think there are some human beings who radiate influence?"

An eminent Parisian doctor said to a number of other physicians around him: "I have completely adopted the ideas of Mr. Coué."

A polytechnician, known as a severe critic, says of Mr. Coué: "He is a power."

Yes; he is a power for good; without mercy for the bad autosuggestions of the "defeatist" type, but indefatigably active, painstaking and smiling, he is at all times ready to help everyone to develop his or her personality. Finally he teaches them how to *cure themselves*; these are the beneficial characteristics of the Coué "method."

How could one fail to desire, from the very bottom of one's heart, that *all* might understand and seize the good news which Mr. Coué brings. It is the *awakening*, possible for everyone, of the personal power to be healthy, successful and happy. It is, if you consent, the full development of a power which may transform your whole life.

Therefore, it is the privilege and the duty of the initiated to spread, by every possible means, the knowledge of this wonderful "method," the happy results of which have been recognized and testified to by many thousands of persons. Such testimony will teach other thousands of people who suffer, who are in pain and in tears, ready to despair. Help them all to get the benefits of this practice.

Then, thinking of France, triumphant but bruised; of her defenders, victorious but mutilated; of all the physical and mental suffering caused by the war; may those who have the power ("the greatest power ever given to man is the power of doing good"—*Socrates*) see to it that this inexhaustible source of mental and physical force which the *Coué* "*method*" puts within the reach of every one, becomes the patrimony of the entire nation and, through it, of all humanity.

MME. EMILE LEON,
Collaborator, at Paris, of *Mr. Coué*

Conclusion

What *conclusion* is to be drawn from all this?

The conclusion is a very simple one and can be expressed in a few words: We possess *in ourselves* an *incalculable force* which is often prejudicial to us, if we handle it unconsciously. If, on the contrary, we direct it in a *conscious and wise* manner, *it gives us the mastery of ourselves* and enables us, not only to save ourselves from physical and mental ills and ailments, but also to help others; and to live in comparative happiness under any and all conditions.

Last but not least, *suggestion* and *autosuggestion* should be used for the moral regeneration of those who have strayed from the right path.

EMILE COUÉ.

How to Practice
Conscious Autosuggestion

Every morning on awakening and every evening as soon as you are in bed, close your eyes, and without fixing your attention on what you say, pronounce twenty times, just loud enough so that you may hear your own words, the following phrase, using a string with twenty knots in it for counting:

"Day by Day, in Every Way, I am Getting Better and Better."

The words: *"In every way"* being good for anything and everything, it is not necessary to formulate particular autosuggestions.

Make this autosuggestion with faith and confidence, and with the certainty that you are going to obtain what you desire.

Moreover, if during the day or night, you have a physical or mental pain or depression, immediately affirm to yourself that you are not going to *consciously* contribute anything to maintain that pain or depression, but that it will disappear quickly. Then isolate yourself as much as possible, close your eyes, and pass your hand across your forehead if your trouble is mental, or over the aching part of your body if your trouble is physical, and repeat quickly, moving your lips, the words: *"It passes, it passes,"* etc. Continue this as long as may be necessary, until the mental or physical pain has disappeared, which it usually does within twenty or twenty-five seconds. Begin again every time you find it necessary to do so.

Like the first autosuggestion given above, you must repeat this one also with absolute faith and confidence, but calmly, without effort. Repeat the formula as litanies are repeated in church.

EMILE COUÉ.

Suggested List

OF STANDARD WORKS ON AUTOSUGGESTION,
PSYCHOLOGY AND OTHER ALLIED SUBJECTS.

ADLER, Dr. Alfred.—The Neurotic Constitution

ARNOLD-FOSTER, M. L.—Studies in Dreams

BALDWIN, James M.—Mental Development in the
    Child and the Race

BAUDOUIN, Charles.—Suggestion and Autosuggestion

BETTS, G. H.—The Mind and Its Education

BRIDGER, A. E.—Minds in Distress

BRILL, Prof. A. A.—Fundamental Conceptions of
    Psychoanalysis

BROOKS, C. Harry.—The Practice of Autosuggestion
    by the Method of Emile Coué

BROWN, H.—Advanced Suggestion

BROWN, W.—Psychology and Psychotherapy

CORIAT, Isador H.—Repressed Emotions

DEWEY, J.—Human Nature and Conduct

DREVER, J.—Psychology of Every Day Life

EDSON, D. O.—Getting What We Want

FIRTH, V. M.—Machinery of the Mind

FREUD, Prof. Sigmund.—Delusions and Dreams.
     With an Introduction by Dr. G. Stanley Hall
FREUD, Prof. Sigmund.—Interpretation of Dreams
FRINK, H. W.—Morbid Fears and Compulsions
GENTILE, G.—Theory of Mind as Pure Act
HEALY, W.—Mental Conflicts and Misconduct
HOBHOUSE, L. T.—Mind in Evolution
HOLLINGWORTH, H. L.—Vocational Psychology
JAMES, W.—Psychology; Advanced Course, 2 Vols
JAMES, W.—Psychology; Briefer Course, 1 vol
JAMES, W.—Talks to Teachers on Psychology
JAMES, W.—Collected Essays and Reviews
JUNG, C. G.—Psychology of the Unconscious
KITSON, H. D.—How to Use Your Mind
KULPE, Oswald.—Outlines of Psychology
LAY, W.—Man's Unconscious Spirit
LAWRENCE, D. H.—Psychoanalysis and the
     Unconscious
LEVY, P. E.—Rational Education of the Will
MARSHALL, H. R.—Mind and Conduct
MERCIER, Chas.—Sanity and Insanity
MOLL, Dr. Albert.—Hypnotism
MUNSTERBURG, Hugo.—Psychology: General and
     Applied
MYERSON, A.—Foundations of Personality
PIERCE, F.—Our Unconscious Mind and How to Use It
PRINCE, M.—The Unconscious
QUACKENBOS, J. D.—Body and Spirit
RUSSELL, B. A. W.—Analysis of Mind
SEASHORE, C. E.—Psychology in Daily Life

STEKEL, Dr. Wilhelm.—The Beloved Ego
STOUT, G. F.—Analytic Psychology; 2 Vols
TANSLEY, A. G.—The New Psychology and Its
        Relation of Life
TITCHENER, E. B.—An Outline of Psychology
TITCHENER, E. B.—Experimental Psychology. Vol. 1,
        Qualitative Experiments: Pt. 1 Student's
        Manual; Pt. 2 Instructor's Manual
TITCHENER, E. B.—Experimental Psychology. Vol. 2,
        Quantitative Experiments: Pt. 1 Student's
        Manual; Pt. 2 Instructor's Manual
TITCHENER, E. B.—A Beginner's Psychology
TRIDON, A.—Psychoanalysis, Sleep, and Dreams
VARENDONCK, Dr. J.—The Psychology of Day
        Dreams. Introduction by Prof. Sigmund Freud
WATTS, Frank.—Echo Personalities
WHITE, W. A.—Mechanisms of Character Formation
WUNDT, W. M.—Lectures on Human and Animal
        Psychology
WUNDT, W. M.—Ethical Systems

Coué League of America

I n France, and various countries of Europe where the earliest benefit of Mr. Coué's clinics was naturally felt, there came an early demand for an organization to unite those who were sympathetic with this wonderful work, and the Lorraine Society of Applied Psychology resulted; and now, in America, a very great interest has developed which is demanding a form of organization. In this busy day many of the best things slip into the background of our thought, and are practically lost to us. It must not be so with this. The need is so great and the "Method" so scientific, practical and efficient that we should make the most of it, for ourselves and others. The remoteness of France and the difference of language seemed to make a separate organization desirable in this country and therefore a number of persons have united in forming the "COUÉ LEAGUE OF AMERICA." Anyone may become a member of the "LEAGUE" by registering his or her name and address, thus expressing an interest in the Coué Ideal of SELF MASTERY by AUTOSUGGESTION.

This is not primarily an organization of the sick or those who have been cured—though all such are of course welcomed—but any who see in the "method" an opportunity of benefitting practically and actually in soul, mind and body, are invited to unite with the "COUÉ LEAGUE OF AMERICA." That such benefit is within the reach of all will, I think, be realized by any who give reasonable thought to this little book.

Those who read this volume with care, will realize that Mr. Coué is merely introducing and out-lining a very large subject. Much has been written upon the subject already, and there will doubtless be presented in the future many volumes, lectures, discussions, etc. Appended to this announcement will be found a bibliography of works now existing. We will be glad to furnish any one with copies of these books at current prices. We also plan to keep the members of the League in touch with the advance which may be made in the subject in future works.

A course of lectures is now being prepared which promises to be helpful. The lectures are designed to extend the principles of Mr. Coué into several fields of interest which are merely suggested in this little volume, but are not carried out in any detail. Information as to this course of lectures will be furnished on request.

It is our conviction, that this movement, initiated by Mr. Coué is destined to have wide influence and useful-